WHO DO YOU THINK YOU ARE?

How to Build Self-Esteem

WHO DO YOU THINK YOU ARE?

How to Build Self-Esteem

Joel Wells

THE THOMAS MORE PRESS
Chicago, Illinois

Grateful acknowledgment is made to the following for permission to include copyrighted material:

Excerpt from *Co-Dependent No More* by Melody Beattie. Copyright © 1987 by the Hazeldon Foundation. Reprinted by permission of Harper & Row, Inc.

Excerpt from *Honoring the Self* by Nathaniel Brandon. Jeremy P. Tarcher, Inc., Los Angeles, CA. Copyright © 1983 by Nathaniel Brandon. Reprinted by permission of St. Martin's Press, Inc.

ISBN 0-88347-240-6 (paper)

ISBN 0-88347-243-0 (hardcover)

Contents

For the Staff of
THE THOMAS MORE ASSOCIATION

"Nobody can make you feel inferior
without your consent."

Eleanor Roosevelt

Introduction

W E are what we pretend to be," according to Kurt Vonnegut, Jr. And that is too bad, because what many people pretend to be is a lot less unique, capable, lovable and happy than they could be if only they would stop pretending.

To pretend is to escape reality, to play a role written by somebody else. In our daydreams and fantasies it is true that we may be the author but in real life our self-image is almost always dictated by others, put together over the years in bits and pieces. Parents, childhood play and schoolmates, teachers, relatives, athletic coaches, friends, fellow workers, bosses, even ministers, priests and rabbis all contribute.

If the resulting composite self-image is positive, powerful, accepting, unassailed by doubts, you are very fortunate indeed. If it is weak, negative, hateful, rejecting, then you are in trouble because it is an almost automatic reflex to equate self-esteem, self-worth, with a self-image that for the most part has been absorbed from others.

It is the aim of this book to convince those who are plagued with a shaky self-image and overall negative feelings (everybody has a less than admirable view of some aspect of "me" but they do not let it run or ruin their life) that you are being needlessly victimized by somebody who should be your best friend and admirer—namely, yourself. Or to put it the way it really is, your self-image is running roughshod over your *real self*, a self that is as good as anybody else's, a self you probably have not encountered, much less appreciated, since it began to take a beating in childhood and which has been understandably hiding out in the dusty attic of your memory.

The result is a gradual self-alienation—so gradual, perhaps, and so long-standing that you do not even realize that you have grown into accepting somebody that is not you. In her fine book, *Codependent No More* (Harper & Row), Melody Beattie describes the sort of trap we can get into if we surrender completely: "We don't like the way we look. We can't stand our bodies. We think we're stupid, incompetent, untalented and, in many cases, unlovable. We think our thoughts are wrong and inappropriate. We think our feelings are wrong and inappropriate. We believe we're not important, and even if our feelings aren't wrong, we think they don't *matter*. We're convinced our needs aren't important. And we shame someone else's desires or plans. We think we're inferior to and different than the rest of the world—not unique, but oddly and inappropriately different. We have never come to grips with ourselves, and we look at ourselves not through rose-colored glasses but through a dirty, brownish-gray film."

There are many admirable and learned psychological and psychiatric books, theories and studies available to the reader who is diligent and patient

Who Do You Think You Are?

enough to go that route to recovering self-esteem. And it is true that both motivation and some grinding reassessment and repair work will be required to retrieve it. For one thing, it involves confronting realities that may be painful to accept and then accepting them anyway—with a new-found self-compassion. As Kermit the Frog says, "It's not easy being green." But it is as useless for Kermit to pretend that he is not green as it is foolish for him to think less of himself because he is.

So here, in the most direct language I can muster, is a guide to getting back in touch with the real you, a you that can accept and go with who you really are to a fuller, happier life—one in which pretending is no longer necessary.

For who you think you are does, in fact, make all the difference.

CHAPTER ONE
In the Beginning

Baby Patrick's project for the day is to pull himself up the side of his playpen and grab the railing. He is already pretty good at sitting up but when he faces the vertical bars they are too far away to reach. He lunges and smacks his head on a bar. After repeating this mistake two more times he scrunches sideways and gets a grip on a bar and pulls himself up by one arm until he tilts sideways and falls down with his nose between two bars.

His older sister watches and laughs. This does not bother Patrick. He tries and falls again, and again. He wets his diaper. His nose is running. He is clumsy.

His sister says, "You'll never do it, you silly baby. You're too little to do that yet."

Patrick doesn't understand her, he doesn't understand that he looks ridiculous, that he's chubby, that his legs are bowed and his ears stick out. Patrick keeps right on trying. His mother comes in, changes his diaper and puts him down for a nap. When he wakes up and finishes his bottle, Patrick resumes his assault on Everest. Late in the afternoon, just when his sister is passing by his playpen, Patrick makes it. There he stands—or clings—triumphant.

Patrick is very pleased with himself.

BABIES are born shameless. They simply do not care what other people think about them. They have no sense of self-esteem but when you are the center of the universe you do not need self-esteem. It's not accurate, however, to say they have no sense of self. They experience themselves purely as body. According to Dr. Nathaniel Brandon, a pioneer in the study of self-esteem, this is what Freud meant when he said that our first ego is a body ego: "Later, as the mind develops, the child learns to relocate the sense of self 'upward': ego and self find their primary location in the mind."

It has been observed that until they are over a year old, a human baby and an infant chimp are equals. Actually, the baby chimp has a considerable edge in dexterity, strength and perhaps even in most sensory and instinctive areas. After that the chimp may continue to hold the lead in many of these areas but the baby's brain is already beginning to open up its bag of tricks. Those first incoherent words, that fumbling manipulation of the fingers opposing the thumb, the ability to look at a picture of a ball and a real ball and make the association, that grin and gurgle which can either be provoked or spontaneous will soon leave the chimp far behind. The day the baby says "me" it is all over.

The Birth of ME

From that "me" moment on, the baby not only enjoys the fantastic superiority of humanity but must start paying the price for being an intelligent, self-reflective, highly adaptable, complexly sensitive creature. Blessed with the gift of language and a growing sense of self-identity—of uniqueness—the baby grows into a child who struggles to place itself in the context of its world. In the beginning, the words of the language can be as confusing and misleading as they are helpful. The child soon learns to augment them with personal "readings" and interpretations of adult body postures, vocal intensity, and facial expressions.

There is a world of difference, little Becky soon learns, between mother's casually uttered, "Becky, get down off that chair!" and mother, her face flushed, her lips pursed, neck taut, eyes glaring, hissing "Becky, get down off that chair this instant!" In neither case does Becky quite know why she can't be on the chair. It is fun to climb up on it and be high; it is fun to see what's on top of the table and, if possible, grab whatever there is to grab. The fact that she could fall and hurt herself, that there are scissors, needles and a pin cushion on the table which could do her grievous harm simply do not compute.

What does register is that this time when she got up on the chair it really upset mother. Mother is angry. Mother is acting like she does not like Becky. Now Becky's whole world depends on mother (and daddy) liking her. It therefore behooves her to get down off the chair. Puzzling, but no great harm done.

But suppose, as is all too often the case with busy parents, mother is tired, frustrated, or talking on the

Who Do You Think You Are?

phone, so she adds a little zinger to the end of her no-nonsense order to get down off the chair: "Shame on you, you naughty girl!" In her mind Becky has still done nothing wrong, and is still without a clue as to why climbing the chair is bad, but mother has supplied a different dimension, a new and alarming factor: there must be something about Becky herself that is bad, and whatever awful thing that shame is. This may (or may not be) the first time that mother has ever been cross with Becky; something about Becky has changed, or is not as good as it was. All of a sudden Becky is not as sure (there was no reason to even think about it) that she can count on mother (and daddy) loving her all the time just the way she is because, the way she is is not altogether pleasing to them. She is bad and shameful.

Becky has just taken her first step down the long road of decreasing self-esteem. A little smudge has suddenly appeared in the mirror of her esteem for herself.

And So It Goes...

From that little acorn of self-doubt, a mighty oak of self-deprecation and eventually even self-hate can grow. It is too bad in a way that memory has to be an integral part of human intelligence. Or at least our accumulating memories of our own failings and shortcomings. It is also too bad that as children—and frequently as adults—we gradually grow able to sort out

19

Joel Wells

the baloney that comes flying through our daily lives from what is true and what matters in everything from gossip to advertising, but remain completely, helplessly naive about any criticisms or aspersions aimed at ourselves.

Tell an eight-year-old that there really is a Santa Claus or that picking up a toad will give him warts, or that watching too much Saturday morning television will turn his brains to mush and he will laugh at you. Tell him that his legs are too skinny, that he is never going to amount to much with his attitude, that he must be stupid because he is not learning his multiplication tables as fast as his older sister did— tell him almost anything negative about himself—true or false—and he will believe it and store it away in the bank-box of his negative self-image for the rest of his life.

What's worse, he will get all these bad images out and count them from time to time. He will use them as excuses to himself for not trying to meet future challenges and expectations. "There's no sense in my thinking about going to college because everybody knows I'm stupid." "No girl will go to the prom with me because I've got skinny legs." Yes, it gets as ridiculous as that. Even more so, because if he would stop and take a look, those skinny eighteen-year-old legs may still be slender but are really quite attractive and in any case, girls do not really think of themselves as going to a prom with a pair of legs. If our anti-hero, or anybody else, really knew what a teen-

20

Who Do You Think You Are?

age girl yearns for in a prom date he might really have something to worry about—but short of being a Matt Dillon or the current gyrating rock star, so would most other males on the planet.

It's for Real

Though oversimplified here, the journey to a negative self-image begins almost before we are aware of ourselves. In the normal course of things it is gradual and almost imperceptible. Most of us ignore the process and may even be skeptical that it is really going on. But it is very real and perhaps because I was working on this book at the time, I caught an instance of it red-handed just recently.

My eighteen-month-old grandson Mikey and I spend a good deal of time together. And yes, I am nuts about him and he knows it. So when his mother came by to pick him up I went out to the car with them to say goodbye. Mikey suddenly bolts from behind the car into the street—a car is coming. His mother yells and goes rigid. I yell at him too and grab him roughly by the arm, pulling him back. In a sort of frenzied and strident duet his mother and I both give him the works: "Don't ever go in the street. . .I've told you before. . .you'll get run over. . .it's bad to run into the street. . .stay on the sidewalk like I told you. . .blah, blah blah!''

Mikey, of course, begins to cry. But he does something else, too. He begins to whack himself on the side of his head with his hand. Why? Because, looking at the incident from his perspective in so far as I was able: here he was simply going around the car to get into his safety seat as usual when suddenly all hell breaks loose for no apparent reason. His grandpa, who had been playing games with him all afternoon, and who had never said a cross word to him before, much less grabbed him and hurt his arm, is joined by his beloved, positively *everything* mother in yelling at him—saying and showing that they do not like him (he cannot make the distinction between himself and what he did). They are making awful faces and saying loud and ugly-sounding, scary words. They call him bad—a word which he has heard and already knows to be something his mother and his daddy and his grandpa do not like. Where did this bad Mikey come from? All of a sudden nobody likes him. Let's get rid of this bad Mikey inside. Hit him and make him go away. Then they will all like him again.

But the bad Mikey will come back. And the good Mikey is already learning to hide him away inside himself. And, if he is really in there, then the good Mikey is not really going to be able to be good all the way through ever again.

There is much food for thought for parents (and grandparents) in all this, but this is not a book about child psychology—it is for adults who have been living with their own bad person for so long that he or she has taken over too much control.

We will be looking at the process that lets this hap-

Who Do You Think You Are?

pen in order to reverse it. Right now it is important to realize that it is real and that it is destructive. Here's how Psychiatrist Theodore I. Rubin, M.D. sums it up in his very insightful book *Compassion and Self-Hate* (Macmillan):

> Once the self-hating process has been set in motion it becomes firmly entrenched and develops an autonomy of its own. It comes to be felt as the central core of one's identification. One sees oneself relative to self-hating values and ideas. Eventually, any feeling or idea about one's self that springs from whatever healthy self-esteem has managed to stay alive is felt as alien and threatening, and poses a threat to a process which like all totalitarian processes, requires *total* subjugation and compliance for survival. Therefore, *any* feelings of real self-esteem or any contribution to real self-esteem are quickly repressed.

CHAPTER TWO
Put-Downs: Their Care and Feeding

*"I have had just about all
I can take of myself."*

S. N. Behrman
(on reaching 75)

COMEDIANS rely on self put-downs. They are funny. We identify with them out of our own intimate knowledge of self-deprecation. Coming from the powerful and the famous they seem delightfully absurd. But there is nothing funny about most self put-downs. And we take no pleasure from the grueling process which first saddles us with them—the put-downs inflicted on us by others.

As noted in the previous chapter, self-awareness begins in innocence—innocence of the sort that it is not burdened by comparisons with any so-called norms, standing free of self-consciousness about shortcomings in appearance, performance, or lovability. The baby neither esteems himself nor rejects himself—he simply is. But other people almost immediately begin to participate in forming his own image of himself in ways mysterious to him, and as time passes, in overtly positive and negative "messages."

The growth of self-awareness becomes hopelessly enmeshed with the sort of self-consciousness which is constantly measuring itself against standards not of one's own making. Gradually a self-image begins to emerge which is a composite of the factual or real self and the self perceived or reflected in the received judgments and assessments of first—as the current phrase has it—"significant others" (parents, grandparents, older sisters and brothers) and then by just plain others—any Tom, Dick or Harriet who wants to give us a pat on the back or a kick in the psyche.

Joel Wells

Varieties of Put-Downs

Put-downs come in all sizes, shapes and flavors. They start coming early in life and continue delivery right into the sunset years. They range the gamut of human vulnerability—physical, emotional, mental, psychological. But they all have one thing in common: each has a barbed stinger which bites in and is terribly hard to remove.

Received Put-Downs

First there are those put-downs which simply seem to envelop us, or that we "receive" like radio signals out of the seemingly clear blue sky of childish life. Those that come early may scarcely be remembered or by now be completely lost to conscious recollection. That does not mean that they did not strike home. Can you remember, as I can, the murmur of adult voices—relatives, friends of your parents—droning on as you were nodding off to sleep in a chair or on a bed in the next room? It went something like this:

"Oh, he's a nice child—but so spindly. Looks like one of those matchstick drawings. He'll get bullied when he starts to school."

"She's a cute little thing except for those squinty eyes."

"He seems smart enough, but if they don't watch it that stammer is going to turn into a full-time stutter."

Who Do You Think You Are?

"They really can't account for that mop of awful red hair. They say that when they go out people look at both of them and then at that carrot top and smile."

"Really, nearly four years old and they still have to put a diaper on him at night."

And then there are parents themselves:

"How many times do I have to tell you? Sometimes I think you haven't a brain in your head."

"Only nasty, dirty children touch themselves there."

"Don't be a pig! I made those cookies for everybody, not just for you."

"Do you do it just to spite me? You give me a headache."

"You're hopeless. I give up."

"You're never going to amount to anything if you don't learn to think about others."

"Quit whining and grow up, why don't you. Nobody likes a crybaby!"

And our darling little playmates (including older brothers and sisters). These are still for the most part the thoughtless, insensitive remarks and observations of small children, not the malicious cruelty of schoolmates. But they are *perceived* as put-downs, nonetheless:

29

"Mommy, why does Janie have those ugly spots on her face and arms?" (Freckles)

"Tommy made a puddle in the hall."

"Why do your ears stick out so far?"

"Can't you even print your name yet?"

"You don't hold it like that, dummy!"

These received put-downs, and scores more, assail our virgin self-image with doubts and worries. At the very best we begin to perceive ourselves as less than perfect, as not measuring up in certain areas of appearance, attitude, abilities, and cleverness which evidently are desirable norms or expectations widely held by others—even those who seem to love us. At worst, they may make us ashamed of being who we are.

But childhood is a pell-mell time. Too much is happening; there is too much to learn and experience; too much excitement and growing to be done to dwell introspectively on these negative images for long. And, with time, many of these received put-downs self-destruct: we no longer wet our pants; we learn how to print our names; we grow less spindly; we see lots of other children with freckles and red hair who don't seem the least upset about either; we see our mothers and fathers blowing up and sounding off about everything from cars that refuse to start to washing machines that overflow and realize that it is not necessarily some fatal flaw in us that brings out such disturbing behavior.

Still, the process has been started. We have learned to doubt ourselves and worse, to accept comparisons and opinions and judgments of others noncritically.

Deliberate Put-Downs

As we grow older received put-downs keep dropping on us, but we also begin to encounter deliberate put-downs aimed at, and specially customized for our non-benefit.

The little girl or boy who is dragged tearfully off to school may be crying because she or he is frightened of the unknown. "Be brave," we tell them, "you do not want the teachers and the other children to think you are still a baby." But even though they cannot articulate their fear, they may be justified in their prophetic tears, because school is where comparisons and competition not only get into high gear but do so under official sanction.

Good teachers are aware of the sensitivity and vulnerability of the rows of little selves arrayed before them. But however tactful they are, bruises, bangs and blows to self-esteem will be inevitable. Some children are brighter than others; some have been tutored by parents and extended family; some are emotionally and physically more mature than others; some have scarcely ever held a book or a pencil in their hands; some have heard nothing but the King's English and impeccable pronunciation since the day they were born, while others have grown up scarcely hearing the language. It is next to impossible to teach this amalgam without making comparisons, without praise, without discipline, without threats. There are gold stars for encouragement and no stars for failures; there are quizzes, tests, grades and report cards; there is rebellion to be curbed, sullenness to be ignored and apathy to be overcome.

This is a challenge to try the patience of a saint, the endurance of an Olympic athlete and the psychological skills of Sigmund Freud. Normal teachers, overworked, in crowded classrooms, underpaid and underappreciated cannot help but generate deliberate put-downs:

"James, everybody else has read out loud today, why can't you?"

"Mary, your desk is as messy as your hair."

"Peter, I know you're short but you can at least sit up straight."

"Janet, look at Susan's drawing and see how it ought to be done."

Put-downs from teachers may not be vicious, but they can sting just as badly because they are given publicly, from on high, in front of everyone. It is as if the recipient has been stamped for all to behold with a sort of "Bad Housekeeping Seal of Disapproval."

Who Do You Think You Are?

Who but the hardiest, supremely confident self could fail to accept the validity of the assessment and its implications—I am dumber than the rest of the class; I am not neat and attractive; I am so short that I must be some sort of freak; I'm a klutz compared to Susan.

And who but Superman or Wonder Woman would say to themselves: never mind what she thinks; I can learn to read as well as anyone; I'll show them what neat and attractive is; I may be short but I'm mighty; Susan's no big deal.

Self Put-Downs

So that is usually how it begins. Even if we don't accept deliberate or received put-downs, they cause us to doubt ourselves in those areas that have been softened up and are now subject to suspicion. Actually, received and deliberate put-downs are painful and embarrassing, but in themselves they really do no permanent harm to anything much but our pride. It is when we nurture them, bring them out and replay them in any threatening or challenging situation, that they turn into self put-downs and become vicious.

Self put-downs are things which we believe to be true about ourselves, whether or not they actually are, and which we allow to dictate both our behavior and sense of worth.

We will be seeing many examples and varieties of self put-downs in the pages that follow. For the moment it is important to remember that they are the ones that take the biggest toll on self-esteem and have drastic and lasting consequences which, for the most part, are totally unnecessary.

Taking but one of the cases just cited, if the deliberate put-down laid so casually on James is taken to heart, it could result in his really thinking he is too "dumb" to try to excell or even keep up in school, forget about going to college since it would be beyond the reach of his feeble brain, and perhaps affect his future job and career potential. All because he felt shy, perhaps, or was unprepared, or daydreaming, or running a fever or was, in fact, having a tougher time learning to read because of a mild dyslexia which he would—in the normal course of things—overcome.

CHAPTER THREE
The Killing Fields of Adolescence

"Actress Kim Basinger, the sassy ex-model who rose to fame in such movies as 'The Natural' and '9 1/2 Weeks,' says she was anything but star material growing up in Athens, Ga.

" 'I had a strange prettiness that was not accepted,' she said in the November issue of Self magazine. 'I was too tall and so uncomfortable around the more boisterous and outspoken girls that my palms were always sweating.'

"And her lips seemed too big, she said. 'I went to school with my hand over my mouth.'

She said she kept her sanity by promising herself, 'I'll get outta here, I'll get outta here!' I talked myself into my own little cult!"

—Chicago Sun-Times

THE deliberate put-downs that hurt the most, and probably have the greatest staying power come from our youthful peers. Whether or not you believe in Original Sin, a good case for its existence can be found in the cruelty of children—and teen-agers—directed at other children.

William Golding's masterpiece, *Lord of the Flies*, is an allegory that combines anthropology and original sin to show how a civilized group of English school boys, stranded on an uninhabited island, quickly revert to primitive, ritualistic savagery. Those who try to resist this descent into darkness are persecuted and shunned. The helpless, myopic fat boy—Piggy—is a focal point of torment.

In real life, of course, things don't go that far but kids will torment and persecute each other with ferocity when the opportunity presents itself. There are many theories as to why this is so, but basically it boils down to "the best defense is a good offense" scenario. If you can pick on somebody else and, if at all possible, enlist the support of others, it diverts attention from yourself and heads off the exposure of and ridicule of your own perceived weaknesses and shortcomings.

All young people feel vulnerable and, beginning with the onset of puberty, are searching for an identity that is distinct from that of simply being part of a family. "Adolescence," says Dr. Theodore Lidz, professor of psychiatry at Yale, "is a time of seeking: a seeking inward to find who one is; a searching outward to locate one's place in life; a longing for another with whom to satisfy cravings for intimacy and fulfill-ment. It is a time of turbulent awakening to love and beauty but also of days darkened by loneliness and despair. It is a time of carefree wandering of the spirit through realms of fantasy and in pursuit of idealistic visions, but also of disillusionment and disgust with the world and self. . . . Adolescents live with a vibrant sensitivity that carries them to ecstatic heights and lowers them to almost untenable depths."

With so much on the line it is difficult to overesti-mate how much put-downs can hurt. Now it is not just one minor flaw or oddity that is being exposed, it is all of you—the whole package. Labels that will last a lifetime are being stuck on you by others and all too often by yourself.

How Shall I Compare Thee?

Adolescence, especially beginning with high school, is the dawning of the age of comparison. First, and most obviously, things physical. You put a bunch of naked fifth or sixth grade boys or girls into a shower and there are not all that many or marked differences to behold. But puberty is not an even-handed mistress. Put the same groups in the same setting three years later and many differences are evident.

We are all too familiar with these to need to rehearse them in detail but boys without hairy chests, fully developed genitals, and muscle bulges have a hard time wishing they were not on display. Girls with more baby fat than breast development feel the same way. Those who are destined to be high school athletes and class beauties make their presence (and relative physical superiority) evident quite soon. High school is a new society especially to freshmen because, aside from the smaller worlds of family and elementary school, it is the only one they have experienced. It seems both endless and unchangeable. They are rapidly caught up in a sort of "pecking order" in which they are assigned a place by virtue of their bodies.

It is the rare teen-aged boy who would not prefer to be big, handsome and athletic rather than the leading brain in his class. And it is the rare teen-aged girl who would not rather be written down as pretty, lithesome and popular rather than, "Well, you really have to get to know her to appreciate how nice she is."

Those on the short end of all these comparisons tend to accept them and define themselves in the terms laid down by this society. "That's who I am, I guess, and how it has to be." Of course, these things no more define their real identity, worth, value or lovability than does some quick cartoon by a second-rate artist. But such is the sensitivity and vulnerability of adolescence.

The Stuff That Dreams Are Made Of

So pervasive and powerful is this perceived pecking order syndrome in high school that—even in my own recollection—I remember boys who had been labeled physical wimps as freshmen still deferring to peers who had been macho men as freshmen and sophomores but who were now relatively puny compared to the hunks that they suddenly turned into between their junior and senior years. Plain Janes who bloomed into beauties went largely unnoticed in the eyes of boys who would have bayed after them lustily if they looked like they looked as seniors when they were freshmen.

I suspect that every reader has his or her own bittersweet emotional diary held over from adolescence and high school. This is the stuff of which fantasies are made—dreams of both glory and revenge; of put-downs shoved back down people's throats and triumphs acted out before a long-gone but still remembered peer group.

The popularity of the rash of high school movies produced in recent years is usually attributed to the fact that as the adult population succumbs to the lures of the VCR and cable television and slides back down the evolutionary ladder into couch-potatodom, teenagers (who have their own reasons for getting out of the house) comprise an ever-larger percentage of the cinema-going audience. But even if adults don't go out to these movies (there was a recent magazine cartoon showing an angry-looking middle-aged man standing under a movie marquee asking the ticket-seller: "Is there anybody over 21 in this picture?") I think they watch them when they come to television

Who Do You Think You Are?

with a secret fascination born of their own adolescent traumas.

In *Carrie*, Sissy Spacek plays a young high school girl who becomes the butt of derision and ridicule by her classmates. She has her first menstrual period in the school shower room and, because her religiously fanatic mother has never told her about such things, she screams in terror, providing further grist for peer persecution. More humiliation and torment follows. But Carrie finds she has a strange telekinetic power which emerges from her beaten subconscious mind— she can make things move and fly and burn. At the movie's climax she exacts terrible and bloody revenge on her classmates—and her mother. Gory as it all is, there were thousands of teen-agers and former teen-agers throughout the world who cheered her on as the cinematic personification of their own revenge fantasies.

Too often, however, these labels linger in our own conscious minds. We resignedly keep our assigned place in that adolescent pecking order. We keep self-images that have no relationship to the reality of our adult reality.

It is too bad, in a way, that we can't all have a secret power, not like Carrie's, but the ability to travel forward in time and attend our twenty-fifth high school reunion on the day after we graduated. If we could, it would work wonders in erasing adolescent labels and myths. Miss Gorgeous who snubbed and scarred you when she refused to accept your prom invitation is now something of a frowzy mouse with a husband with an understandably roving eye. Mr. Basketball Hero, whom all the girls adored, is now already a bit arthritic, which doesn't help him much in his job as a shoe salesman.

More importantly (and less spitefully perceived), is the fact that a number of nerds of both sexes, of which company you may have been a label-carrying member, have not only prospered but have actually grown betterlooking with age. They are the fortunate ones who shook free and reassessed their self-images in terms of reality. There are others, of course, who allowed themselves to become self-fulfilling prophecies—the plump girl who is now off the top end of the scales, the wimp who is still whining and feeling sorry for himself—and others who would not even think about humiliating themselves again by attending a reunion with the same people who put them through pure hell.

I cannot resist getting personal here. When I did, in fact, attend my twenty-fifth high school class reunion, one of the first people I encountered was the one I most hoped wouldn't be there. I had trouble recognizing him because he had evidently shrunk shockingly in size. As I remembered him he was huge compared to the skinny little me who felt compelled to go out for football as a sophomore. I was, of course, relegated to the third team and used as blocking fodder for the first and second squads' drills.

Most often I was the assigned obstacle to be demol-

Who Do You Think You Are?

ished by the varsity right tackle, who blew me away with savage gusto even in non-contact run-throughs. I was skinny but not a masochist, so after several weeks of this punishment I began to take evasive action whenever I recognized that the play that would bring this monster down upon my frame was being called. I would run to the spot where the runner was heading and take my punishment there. I once actually caused a halfback to fall because he tripped over my supine form.

This caught the eye of the coach who immediately chastized the right tackle for missing his block. He did so with great tact: "If you can't even handle Wells, what are you going to do with a real linebacker?"

After the next play the tackle took advantage of the settling dust to grip me by the throat, threaten me with assault after practice if I so much as tried to move away from my assigned position and punched me in the stomach by way of preview of what would happen if I failed to comply.

I write about it lightly, but it was a shameful and shaming experience—both the pummeling and the put-down by the coach in front of a group I very much wanted to be accepted by. Worst of all it made me feel like a coward because I was in fact afraid to punch the big guy back. I had little choice but to translate it into a self put-down which has made me accept myself as a physical coward for all these years.

And here he was smiling in my face at the reunion, only now he was no larger than I was. Half of me wanted to take advantage of this catching up on my part and smack him in the mouth. But, of course, I didn't and he evidently had no recolleciton of the incident. He greeted me warmly as though we were long-lost friends and spoke of visiting me when he next came to Chicago. And, strangely, it made me feel better about myself; as if an old ghost had finally been laid to rest or at least cut down to size.

Still on a personal note, I was later invited to give the graduation address at my high school. Remembering the utter apathy with which most such commencement talks are received by the students, I was determined to keep it light and lively. I can't say whether I succeeded, but I did sense that I had gotten their attention when I noted that a commencement was not just a beginning but an end—an end to the high school peer world and an end to the pecking order society. Class goats no longer had to think of themselves that way; conversely, athletic stars and "Miss Popularities" would no longer receive automatic star status in the eyes of the world at large which they would be entering. The slate would be wiped clean—and they could commence being who they really were and wanted to be.

It was a nice observation and I hope some of them took it to heart. But I am sure that for all too many, the old self-image held on for dear life.

CHAPTER FOUR
The Real Self Versus Self-Image

*"You can't depend on your eyes
when your imagination is out of focus."*

Mark Twain

THE real self is actually quite simple. It accepts the facts of life as they are. Our friend Baby Patrick would personify these facts if he was capable of thinking about them: *I am alive. I am me; I like being me simply because of who I am; I want to grow, learn, experience love and be happy.*

Simple as it sounds it is actually a very big concept. It embraces the fantastic fact of human existence—a one-of-a-kind existence, because not even identical twins are exactly alike. And twins get differentiated in many nonphysical ways as well. It also embraces a sense of individual worth, hopes, and the quest for fulfillment and happiness. If it truly were a simple, automatic concept to grasp, why do so many of us let our real selves get smothered, lost, abandoned in the course of pursuing what we imagine to be a far more exalted image of self, or a far inferior and hateful image of self.

We will come back to the concept of real self again, but for now its basic importance needs to be held onto as a contrast to any sort of self-image that leads us too far away from the profoundly important perception of who we think we are versus who we really are.

Catch-22

It is easy enough to sound the alarm about the perils of letting a negative self-image, or an unrealistically inflated one (we all know the type who thinks he is God's gift to women, or a know-it-all woman who needs a final filter on her mouth) overpower our real self. But the catch is that it takes a mature and confident sense of true self to resist both the blandishments and the destructive forces that assail it throughout life. In other words, it is terribly hard to develop that hardy sense of true self with so many monkeys on our backs.

Human beings are so susceptible to praise and criticism that both get blown out of all proportion. We start out in life wanting to please and to be accepted. But, as Bill Cosby says, "I don't know the key to success, but the key to failure is trying to please everybody." So when we inevitably fail, we look for a reason. If we cannot find one that makes sense, we first doubt, then blame ourselves. If it is not something we did or did not do, then it must be because we are less than perfect and, in some way we cannot understand, we fail to measure up to the expectations of others.

Great Expectations

French philosopher Jean Paul Sartre wrote that "hell is other people." It is a harsh saying but quite true. If there were no other people in the world to whom we could compare ourselves we would have no reason to think we are not perfect. If there were no other people in the world to create a consensus about what defines beauty, great art, achievement, brilliance, success and happiness, we would have no reason to think that we fall short in possessing or realizing any of them.

But, of course, there are other people and a culture of consensus about all these things in which we must live. It is a world in which it is next to impossible not to make continual self-comparisons and measurements against the models of perfection and achievement which the culture holds up before our eyes and egos. This is life. This is, for better or worse, reality. What is not real is to enter this reality, this life of constant comparisons, with the warped conviction that anything less than perfection is terrible.

And that is precisely what our particular culture seems bent on selling us. Selling us in both the theoretical sense and in the concrete. You cannot sell makeup, hair dyes, deodorants, diet pills, plastic surgery, toupees, workout equipment, elevator shoes, baldness cures, and cosmetic dentistry to gods. Granted, people have been making comparisons ever since Adam noticed something different about Eve, but for most of history people struggled along without fashion magazines, television and other mass media—yes, even advertising.

Not only are we bombarded with perfection images and made to feel that anything less is unacceptable, but we are subtly and not so subtly made to feel guilty about not doing something to achieve perfection. We devalue ourselves by the degree which we fall short. Along with this come two other maxims of conven-

Joel Wells

tional wisdom that we hold sacred—acceptance and perfection must be earned and failure and lack of perfection deserve punishment. Neither is true, but that does not prevent us from building our self-image and our outlook on life on these false premises.

Self-image is a complex whole but it is useful, if we are to be able to separate who we *think* we are from who we *really* are, and to break that whole down into parts.

Body Self-Image

We all have one. It is perhaps the cornerstone of self-image because it tends to condition how we present ourselves to the world and, often, what we think we can accomplish professionally, who we can establish personal and social relationships with, and be either a boost or a drag on other areas of self-esteem: "I may not have the best job in the world, but with my looks people envy me, anyway"; "Yes, people praise my writing, but they still see me as ugly."

In the previous chapter we saw how crucial body self-image is to adolescents and how the put-down process gnaws away at self-esteem. Low physical self-esteem forces people to settle for less—often so much less that it blights their lives.

To take an obvious, but common example, there is the bright, personable girl who is genetically programmed to be heavy-set—not fat but not what the culture has dictated feminine perfection should be.

Who Do You Think You Are?

She picks up plenty of received put-downs to this effect, and in high school some deliberate ones as well. She sees herself as hopelessly unattractive to the opposite sex. She goes dateless through school. She decides that since even when she looks her best it seems to make no difference, she might as well at least have the consolation of eating all she wants. She becomes grossly obese.

Out of school, she looks for work. She figures her appearance rules out jobs that she would be good at—sales, reception, anything that might exploit her special talent for getting along with people—and settles for the impersonal, almost invisible position as a data inputter. Hidden away from public view and possible ridicule behind her computer, she is miserable but safe.

Then to her amazement a man comes on to her at the deli during lunch hour. He is not much to look at, but he is a man and she is no position to be choosy.

From here on her life plays itself out like a bad soap opera. The guy is the worst sort of louse and leech. He has no steady job. He moves into her apartment, spends her hard-earned money on clothes, runs her already failing used car into the ground, gets her pregnant, periodically beats her up, and comes around only when he needs a place to crash.

To compound matters, not only does our girl feel confirmed in her disastrously negative body self-image, she now feels a fool for doubting it for even an instant and for letting herself be used even though she knew what would happen. She will dig deeper and deeper into her shell of misery to make doubly sure that such self-deception and humiliation will never be able to touch her again.

She demonstrates two of the points made above: she accepted a culturally imposed idea of perfection as her standard—a false one about what constitutes feminine attractiveness (A few centuries ago, when women with a little meat on their bones were considered great beauties, she could have posed for Rubens.) Secondly, she equated her only moderate departure from this false perfection with a total failure in personal attractiveness. She let it dictate her whole, horribly negative body self-image.

There are dozens of variations on this theme and they are lived out by men as well as women. There are other scenarios being played out that are less obvious, less tragic, but which nonetheless take their toll.

Body Obsession

In his satiric novel, *Bonfire of the Vanities*, Tom Wolfe describes a party in a high-rise condo peopled by rich and socially ambitious Manhattanites. There are the be-tuxed men of all ages, some accompanied by far younger beauties who are their mistresses, but for the real wife, thirty-five and up, there was only one way to look—starved to a stylish gauntness that would enable her to squeeze into a designer gown.

Who Do You Think You Are?

She seems so unnaturally thin that one could almost see right through her. Wolfe gives these women a generic name: "X-Rays."

In her book *Transforming Body Image: Learning to Love the Body You Have* (Crossing Press), Dr. Marcia Hutchinson, a psychologist who also conducts body image workshops, writes that "the inability to feel at home in our bodies can make life miserable on every front."

In an interview with the *New York Times* she says that the problem is more severe among women—65 percent of whom she estimates are unhappy with their bodies—because the majority of men in our culture are taught—and believe—that their worth is measured by their accomplishments, while women seem conditioned to believe that their social value is hinged to physical attractiveness.

And this new mandate to be slim, fit and muscular (maybe even to the degree of Tom Wolfe's X-Rays) has added a tyrannical imperative to an already impossible mission. There is absolutely nothing wrong with wanting to be fit, to eat and exercise for reasons of health, but to make the X-Ray look the goal is to spend a lot of time and energy uselessly.

"We are so busy obsessing over what is wrong with us," says Dr. Hutchinson, "whether it's our weight, misproportions, wrinkles, pimples, excess hair or functional limitations—that we fail to develop our potential as human beings."

Body Self-Image can be changed and we will be

Joel Wells

looking at ways to do that further on. But by way of contrast to the negative examples we have seen, here's an upbeat flip side of the picture presented by *New York Times* columnist Jane E. Brody:

> One of my most beautiful friends is hardly what our society would call a classic beauty. At five feet, four inches tall and 120 to 125 pounds, she is absolutely average, statistically speaking. Clearly, she is not centerfold material: her belly protrudes a bit, her waist and neck are somewhat foreshortened, her thighs are slightly flabby and her face is round but lacks the delicacy of a cherub.
>
> Yet nearly all who know her see her as beautiful. Why? Because she sees herself as an attractive woman who looks good for her forty years. She is pleased with her physical persona and it shows in how she walks, talks, dresses, laughs and listens. Her dazzling smile projects beauty from the inside out.

As Jane Brody concludes, millions of Americans, especially those men and women who regard their physical selves with disdain, could learn a lot from her friend.

It might also help all those who suffer from a negative body self-image to get things back into a more realistic perspective if they would reflect on some famous people—real and fictional—who depart from the culturally dictated ideals of physical beauty and perfection in some pretty substantial ways, but who do not or did not for a moment let it ruin their lives.

Who Do You Think You Are?

Famed Greek orator Demosthenes had a speech impairment.

Julius Caesar suffered from epilepsy.

At five feet, six inches, Napoleon Bonaparte felt he was too short.

George Washington had false teeth.

Abraham Lincoln thought he was ugly.

Franklin Delano Roosevelt spent most of his adult life in a wheel chair.

Jimmy Durante's nose was preposterously large.

Mohandas Gandhi was a scrawny little man.

Pope John XXIII was built like a beer keg.

Golda Meir was no beauty; neither is Mother Teresa.

Jackie Kennedy worried that her breasts were too small.

Luciano Pavarotti is fat.

As noted, body self-image is a major component of the complex and hard-to-grasp whole that is our overall self-image. But, as we shall see in the next chapter, it is by no means the only component.

CHAPTER FIVE
Other Components of Self-Image

Peer Gynt: "Who are you?"

The Voice: "Myself.
Can you say as much?"

Henrick Ibsen

BEST-selling books hit the top of the chart and presently disappear into the relative obscurity of library stacks. Other books that never appear on the lists are the real all-time best sellers—the Bible, for instance. But there are dozens of children's books that live on and on, as well. One of these is the beloved story of "The Little Engine That Could." Kids love it first of all because they identify with the littleness of the engine and rejoice when it is able to accomplish what the big and powerful engine cannot. Parents keep on buying the book for their children because they see it as an effective dramatization of what willpower and a positive attitude can accomplish.

And that it certainly is. Even though the engine was little, and knew itself to be little, it was determined. It is the rare young reader who fails to join in chanting the familiar refrain puffing out of the smokestack of the little engine as it labors up the mountain pulling its heavy load: "I think I can. . .I think I can. . .I think I can." And then as it nears the top: "I know I can. . .I know I can." Finally, triumphantly going down the other side of the mountain: "I knew I could. . .I knew I could."

For our purposes, the Little Engine That Could has a realistic and positive self-image and is thus able to perform up to the maximum of its potential—and not only get the job done, but feel even better about itself—happy and fulfilled.

But, as we look at some other aspects of self-image, it may be useful to contrast the attitude of the Little

Joel Wells

Engine That Could with unrealistic expectations or undeserved limitations which we let our self-image dictate. In effect, these are making us think and say to ourselves: "I know I can't. . .What's the use. . .I won't even try."

Intellectual Self-Image

In addition to Body self-image, a critical component of our overall self-image is how intelligent we perceive ourselves to be. Here comparisons may be more relative than with body self-image. That is, while the standards of physical perfection dictated by our culture seem fairly uniform and preposterously high, there is not the same sort of universal expectation that every one of us must either be a genius or consider ourselves idiots if we fall below that mark.

For one thing, intelligence is not physically visible in the way that good looks are. To use the chauvinistic cliche, a dumb blond is just a blond until she opens her mouth. Another: most adults get through much of their lives without having to expose their ignorance. Most of us know our specific shortcomings or blank spots and admit them.

"I never was any good at math."

"I simply can't get my tongue around a foreign language."

"Trying to express myself in writing ties me up in knots."

"Me, read music? You've go to be kidding."

And these are good, honest adult admissions. They

Who Do You Think You Are?

are things we have learned to accept about ourselves without necessarily letting them lower our self-esteem.

But it is not quite that easy when we are children. As we have seen, that is when received and deliberate put-downs may take their terrible toll on self-esteem. Here we are not dealing with the learning gaps and specific learning difficulties of the paragraph above. When we take a mental put-down to heart as a child, it may well grow into the sort of mental self-image that tells us we are, if not stupid, certainly inferior, below the norm in intelligence, that we will have to limit our expectations about learning, and ultimately, perhaps, about the sort of work or career we are capable of pursuing with any reasonable hope of success.

Stupid is as stupid does, the saying goes. But what is really stupid and tragic is that we attach such a label to a mind that could in all probability grow and function more than adequately. There is an almost tangible power at work here. When the child, or teen-ager, or adult who has a negative mental self-image finds himself or herself facing a mental challenge of any sort—a test, a book report or essay to be written, the prospect of a demanding college course (or higher education itself), or a job which entails learning complex routines—panic sets in. It is as if a curtain drops before their interior eyes. All begins to turn into a muddle. They may even sweat and experience an increased pulse rate. What they do not realize is that most people experience this panic when faced with a mental challenge, but that many have learned by experience that it can be quelled and penetrated; that beyond that curtain—perhaps a mental sound barrier is a better analogy—things become peaceful, the brain resumes its mysterious functioning and the challenge falls into pieces which can be dealt with step at a time.

As with the case of actors who experience stage fright, or speakers whose mouths grow dry at the prospect of the open microphone before them, one has to plunge ahead. After you have made the plunge once, twice, a dozen times, mental confidence begins to shred the curtain to tatters and perhaps makes it disappear forever.

Sometimes the opposite is true. There are many cases when a mental self-image can be falsely pumped up through early praise and easy achievement only to come a cropper in later life. More than one quick learner who breezed through elementary school and had little difficulty in a relatively small and undemanding high school, enters college thinking he is going to eat the place alive. But thrown into demanding courses, with no study habits or any experience of hard mental exercise, competing with peers who are armed with these tools and every bit as bright, our whiz kid with his hulking mental self-image is getting sand kicked in his face.

Social Self-Image

Our total self-image is also composed of a number of other factors that contribute to the person we think

Who Do You Think You Are?

we are. Some of these are hard to define and may overlap a bit, so let us lump them under the heading social, since they all relate to perceptions and comparisons made between ourselves and other people.

The United States boasts of being a classless society. We admit to economic distinctions such as lower, middle and upper class, but in our working democracy, founded on the premise that all people are created equal, we allow no kings or queens, no dukes or duchesses, no earls, barons, lords or knights. Unlike India we have no caste system, no Brahmins or Untouchables. We may have blue and white-collar workers, middle management and upper echelon executives. But in theory, at least, we don't, as England is supposed to perpetuate, have a fixed working or lower class, and an entrenched educated or elite class, with a social iron curtain separating the two.

Perhaps not, but we have managed to sort ourselves out and position ourselves up or down on a social ladder, the rungs of which are supposed to define our status, and thus to an extent our worth. Some of these distinctions were far more potent in our recent past than they are today. The White Anglo-Saxon Protestant (WASP)'s perceived social superiority over Jews and Catholics has largely eroded as have many of the automatically limiting ethnic labels of an immigrant population as group after group moves into the American mainstream. There is still plenty of racism to go around, however, and it is always a social tragedy when a person is made to think less of himself or herself because of skin color or religious beliefs.

Joel Wells

But we also have a lot of handy social labels to stick on people—redneck, good-old-boy, YUPPIE, gay, mid-westerner, jock, Valley girl, Jewish princess, farm boy, ghetto rat—which seldom are heard as encouraging words. Still, it is not these verbal stones which break the bones of our cultural self-image. Many of those who are so pegged wouldn't have themselves any other way. What hurts is to feel trapped by social circumstances which demean your worth in the eyes of others and yourself. Poverty is one of these circumstances. Lack of opportunity is another—the opportunity to get a decent education, to learn to read and write effectively, to speak without betraying these social handicaps, to find a decent job that offers a measure of self-respect.

Too many bright, potentially hard-working, creative people have been frustrated by the low place on the social ladder in which they find themselves. It is true that they are unjustly deprived but they should not lower their self-esteem, nor be forced to give up hope on that account. If it is society that robs the great and growing underclass in our so-called classless country of any sense of self-worth, then it is society that should be gravely concerned about making it possible for people to begin to build the sort of social self-image that can lead them out of the crushing cycle of poverty.

Forgive the editorializing, but by comparison to our own second nation of deprived and homeless, and to the terribly inhuman conditions which exist in the

Who Do You Think You Are?

Third World, the problems which beset the social self-image of the rest of us seem trivial by comparison. They are there, nonetheless:

People who make less money than their friends wonder why.

Some people are ashamed of their parents, their perceived lesser social lineage.

Others worry about their lack of taste in clothes, home decor, and artistic taste.

There are those who dread parties, teas, receptions—any place where they must mingle with strangers. They are at a loss for small talk, they feel insecure, unimportant, embarrassed and uncomfortable.

Many wear a continual no-nonsense mask of intensity and seriousness to conceal the fact that they have always had trouble understanding or telling jokes or picking up on any sort of irony or humor.

The person who has not gone to college who mingles, works and lives with people who have, will struggle with feelings of inferiority.

So will the person who has gone to a university or college of lesser reputation than his or her colleagues.

People worry about making fools of themselves in matters of grammar, pronunciation, table manners, social protocols involved in engagements, weddings and other such monumental occasions.

Joel Wells

Teen-agers (and their adult counterparts) can grow so preoccupied about appearing in the right place in the wrong clothing that they grow physically ill.

Social self-image is also tied very closely to the sort of work we do, the profession we follow, the life-style we are able to afford and follow, what our children amount to, and a host of other factors. Occupational status, in particular, plays a dominant role in our social self-image. So much so that it overlaps into the related but more powerful area of identity definition, which will be discussed a bit later.

Psychological Self-Image

In a sense the whole concept of self-image is psychological—in our head. Here it is used as a category for those areas of self-perception which reflect on certain intangible but important attitudes, capabilities, dispositions with which we customarily deal with problems and with other people.

Do you regard yourself as tough-minded, for instance? A realist who sees through much of the malarky which our mass media and politicians put out as the gospel truth? The sort of person who knows how to deal with car and insurance salesmen? A woman or man who isn't afraid of a little confrontation—and in fact may relish it.

Or do you view yourself as a meeker sort, one who dreads tangling things up verbally, hates arguments, and will, given the chance to keep things peaceful, take the line of least resistance?

Do you regard yourself as capable, a problem-solver, a manager possessed of enough self-confidence to handle almost any problem? Or does the unexpected always tend to throw you for a loop—frazzle your brain, so that you find it more comfortable to play things the safe, routine way?

Are you the patient, calm sort who can hear people out and see crises through or do you tend to blow up and go to pieces?

Are you the sort of person who cannot stand to be alone or one who needs a daily fix of solitude to keep on an even keel?

Do you have difficulty controlling your temper or do you tend to bottle up your anger and express it in other ways?

Are you vindictive, driven by a passion to get revenge at any cost or do you tend to forgive, even though you may never forget?

All of these questions (there are scores more) have been answered and stored in your psychological self-image. They play a crucial role in determining how you will act and react in daily life.

Sexual Self-Image

Closely related to psychological self-image is the way we view ourselves as sexual beings. While body self-image may increase or diminish the physical assessment we make of how sexy we are, there is a deeper sense in which we view our sexuality.

At its most basic it rests on our acceptance and comfort in being male or female. Do we see ourselves as capable of loving and being loved? Do we rejoice in our sexual urges, fantasies and activities or do they make us feel dirty and ashamed?

A twisted sexual self-image, born of received, deliberate and self put-downs, perhaps fostered by deep psychological scarring and even child abuse, can wreak havoc in terms of personal fulfillment and happiness. It should not and does not have to be that way. As professor James Hitchcock says: "If sex has importance and dignity, it is because it is deeply rooted in the human personality. Who we are has a lot to do with our sexuality and how we live it."

In other words, as we shall see, improving overall self-esteem and rooting it in a true and appropriate self-image will inevitably raise our appreciation of our sexual selves as well.

CHAPTER SIX
Are You What You Do?

*"The biggest lie is the lie we tell
ourselves in the distorted visions we
have of ourselves, blocking out some
sections, enhancing others. What
remains are not the cold facts of a
life, but how we perceive them."*

Kirk Douglas

HERE you are at a party at the house down the block. During the spring and summer a number of new people—including you and your family—have moved into the neighborhood and this is an opportunity to get acquainted. After the hostess welcomes you and your wife and takes your hats and coats, she ushers you into the living room and urges you to introduce yourselves to everyone because she has business to attend to in the kitchen.

And so begins the age-old social sniffing ritual. Disgusting as it is, dogs really do have an easier time sorting each other out and, come to think of it, they may not be any more ridiculous than a bunch of two-legged creatures doing the same number with cocktail glasses and teacups gripped tightly in their hands.

"Hello!"

"Nice to meet you."

"We live in the brown shingle house down the street."

Big deal!

What everybody wants to know, of course, is who you are. But nobody ever asks this direct question because it is: 1) too personal and embarrassing; 2) no one is really prepared to answer it; 3) just as nobody wants an honest answer to the question, "How are you?" no one wants to spend the time needed for a full-scale autobiographical sketch; and 4) if you answered the question as it should be answered—"I am me"—you would soon have more than your share of the living room all to yourself.

Joel Wells

The rules of the game call for revelation of identity by indirection, by signals and code words. Actually, it is a bit like playing twenty questions.

"Are you smaller than a breadbox?"

"Yes."

"Are you rectangular?"

"No."

And so on, till we learn that you are round and firm and fully packed with juice. That you are, in fact, an orange.

Have Your Identity Cards Ready

In our society there is one question that we put to strangers as a matter of course. It takes the place of "Who are you?" It is, "What do you do?"

It is in answering the question that self-identity lets it all hang out—and hangs us out to dry for all the world to see.

Because an attorney will respond to it not by saying, "I practice law," but with "I am a lawyer."

"I am a doctor, professor, mechanic, secretary, rabbi, postal worker, golf pro, sales manager, certified public accountant, graduate student, electrical engineer, firefighter, carpenter, investment banker, etc."

Nine times out of ten, people will answer the question, "What do you do?" as if they had been asked, "Who are you?"

Is it just a small distinction or could it be that for

Who Do You Think You Are?

all too many of us, who we are is equated with what we do?

I'm afraid that the answer is an emphatic yes.

Which means that anyone who is not proud, or at least satisfied with what he or she does, who is not happy about the status that society attaches to what they do, is not pleased with their self-image.

The Status Game

In Chapter Four, Dr. Marcia Hutchinson observed that men more than women were conditioned to believe that their social worth hinged on what they accomplished rather than how they looked. That may well be true as a general statement but there are two important distinctions or qualifications that need to be made.

The first is that if men are so conditioned, then they are more likely to have problems with self-esteem when they are in a profession, trade or job in which they cannot take pride, or to which society attaches little or even negative status. And there are a thousand jobs that can be classified like that—jobs that either make one a cog in a machine or require nothing but back-breaking labor or some menial job like washing dishes from which one can take home no affirmation but a numbed brain, aching muscles and a meager pay check.

It is not just physical labor that destroys pride and

Joel Wells

identity—after all, farmers, carpenters, electricians, masons and professional athletes push their bodies to the limit every day and are both proud and fulfilled. It is labor without personal satisfaction, work that offers no pride of accomplishment, no hope of bettering one's lot, putting in time for no goal other than wages, that depersonalizes and destroys the image that is equated with status.

If that is bad, having no job at all is the worst thing for a man, young or old. So is having no recognizable place or face in society at any age. Adolescents who cannot cope with school, and thus can claim no image as a student on the way to somewhere, who no one will hire, who find no warmth or validation in broken or nonfunctioning families—and they are legion—will search out the macho self-esteem of gang membership. Better to be a Cobra or an Avenger, dangerous and desperate as that can be, than to be a nobody. Being faceless, a nonentity in today's society is unbearable.

It is a condition which is far too prevalent, especially in our big cities and one which we would do well to both understand and take steps to reverse.

You have to be *somebody* before you can say no to drugs.

CHAPTER SEVEN
A Woman's Place Is...

*"It is the lack of joy in Mudville,
rather than the presence of sorrow that
makes the difference."*

Dr. June Singer

CHAPTER SEVEN
A Woman's Place

WHAT was described in Chapter Six could be called the Male Identity Crisis. It is both more and less than that. It is more because many women as well as many adolescent girls find themselves in exactly the same unrewarding jobs and faceless roles. It is less because before you have an identity crisis you have to have an identity, and most of the people we have been talking about—men and women—are struggling to find one.

Broad generalizations have a way of sweeping the truth under the rug, but it seems safe to say that contemporary women have been putting their traditional self-images, including the sexual, social and economic roles that our society has assigned to them, under intense scrutiny.

The past three decades have been described as both triumphant and traumatic for women. The feminist movement—deplore it or applaud it as you will—has been, and still is, a social earthquake in progress. The benefits of the sexual revolution are highly debatable, but the movement for equal rights, equal pay, equitable treatment under the law, against sexual harassment and job discrimination by gender—all have shaken and continue to change the social landscape and climate for the better. And there will be no return to the bad old days; there is no way to stop an idea or a cause whose time has come; there is no turning back the hands of a digital clock.

But in the process a very real image crisis has been created for a substantial number of women. It is important and it will be a long time in the resolving.

Joel Wells

Not only have thousands of women entered the work force voluntarily in pursuit of professions and careers in everything from law to firefighting (and many other areas formerly denied them) but hundreds of thousands of others have taken jobs because they are the sole support of their children and themselves. As the cost of living, medical care, and housing have escalated, still other women have either deferred having babies or have placed the ones they have in daycare centers and joined the work force in order to supplement their husbands' income so that the family can remain independent and realize the American dream of owning one's own home.

This has produced tensions and upheavals in all sorts of traditional cultural expectations and roles for contemporary women—and for their husbands and children as well. Men in such matches suddenly find themselves expected to be coparents in a way that they never were before. No longer is it enough for them simply to be the breadwinner and come home to a nice hot meal and a houseful of clean and happy kids who soon drift off to bed.

Now the wife is co-breadearner; she may not get home from work until after he does; the kids need to be picked up from day care and school; somebody has to stand in line at the supermarket, do the laundry, retrieve the drycleaning, pay the bills, get an ailing child to the doctor's office, make the beds, get the car serviced—and so on.

Some men adjust to this and do their fair share in

Who Do You Think You Are?

spite of the fact that their traditional patriarchal status as father-provider-protector is severely diminished. But just as many husbands, even while they grudgingly take up some of the workload of the two-job family, manage to communicate their resentment and unhappiness to their wives, who in turn feel they are not living up to expectations.

Other women do it all themselves. The current label for these tireless hyper-achievers who do everything that the traditional house wife always did while holding down a demanding full-time job is supermom. ("You know the type," cracks comic Carol Leifer: "I just had a baby an hour ago and I'm back at work already. While I was delivering I took a course in tax-shelter options.")

So the stage is set for identity-crises, all accompanied by varying degrees of guilt, self-doubt and possible upsurges or downdrafts of self-esteem. Supermom may well feel pretty good about herself, even as she heads for a possible nervous breakdown. The wife who tries to cope with both job and family and finds herself failing or barely able to hold her own, doubts her worth as a competitor. The wife who stays at home, does all the work and raises the kids may feel she has no status at all.

There are many other variations on the theme which find expression in newspaper columns and magazine articles virtually every day. They are the prime topic for television talk shows, as well, and there even seems to be a new sort of American civil war shaping up as the working moms circle their wagons against the raids of the stay-at-home moms who feel increasingly threatened.

"I go to a party," says Eugenia Geannopoulos, an MBA who gave up a promising career to stay at home and take care of her baby, "and people ask me what I do. When I tell them, they smile at me like I'm an idiot of some sort, or a child, and get away as fast as they can."

Let's listen to 30-year-old Eugenia for a moment because she embodies many of the characteristics of the identity crises which so many young—and not so young—American women are experiencing today. I interviewed her at her home in Portland, Oregon, some months ago while she was confined to bed rest awaiting the birth of her child. But my questions only interrupt her candid self-reflections so I'll omit them.

First Person Singular

"To suddenly abandon a career leaves one with a sense of giving up—of wasting all that you have worked to achieve. I grew up with very specific formulas for success. School and job both provide standards to measure it by. You are graded or ranked with others and you know where you stand—you have an identity, a place in the world that others recognize and respect.

"Once you no longer work, people tend to have a hard time respecting you—probably because they do not understand. It was always very important to me that people respect my intelligence and accomplishments and not just see me as a blond thing with nothing to offer. The minute my career identity was gone I found it harder to relate to people. I already tend to focus on what I used to be in order to establish some rapport with new acquaintances. . . .

"The way one looks is another big part of self-esteem, especially to people like me who have worked hard to try to look and feel my best physically through regular exercise. Now that's gone. Having a child messes with a woman's body in a big way and once the baby arrives there is going to be very little if any time to devote to getting back into shape. It may be selfish, but I want to feel that my husband still finds me attractive and won't be pining away for a firmer, younger-bodied wife.

"But I can feel myself drifting into it—the routine of letting the day go by. Who needs a shower, I can't go out of the house anyway? I'll just leave my sweat suit on all day because it is more comfortable. I dread getting into the frump cycle which will only result in lowering my self-esteem even more.

"My sister says I'm getting too far ahead of reality, as usual. That I am experiencing all the negative things about a hard pregnancy and worrying about all the drawbacks of raising a child without having experienced the real joy of actually having the baby in my arms and in my life.

"Maybe so, but much as we want the baby (it's why

Joel Wells

I quit a very good job just when my prospects for advancement looked great) I realize that these days the challenge of raising children is not perceived as anything special by society. The attitude I pick up is that it doesn't require any unique skills or intellectual strategy; being a mother is viewed as a generic job. If anything, from what I read and see on television, there is a sort of United Union of Mothers who want you to conform and do everything the one RIGHT WAY. I don't want to spend the rest of my days as just another face in the crowd.

"And along with the sense that my special identity is going to be ground away by conformity, I feel guilty about actually not going to work every day as I've been doing ever since George and I got married. I enjoy not having to charge off every morning and not having to take care of household duties during precious time off. But am I really contributing to society in any measurable way? There's no way to measure it but I feel driven to justify my day at home somehow.

"I even feel guilty about worrying about my self at all. Here I sit in a wonderful home, with a wonderful view while my husband has to work extra hard at a new job *and* take care of me. But I am still not sure it is going to be enough to make up for what I've lost—or at least what I think I've lost.

"Regardless of whether there was a career identity before or not, I think most women fear losing themselves completely within childcare. It should not be viewed as a sacrifice but given today's achievement standards and self-expectations, it is hard not to.

Who Do You Think You Are?

"The thought of spending day upon day taking care of babies and then spending hours of socializing devoted to discussing the pros and cons of disposable diapers is terrifying. I'm afraid my mind will turn to mush.

"People say, 'Oh, you will be so busy once the baby comes, you will never be bored.' Busy and bored are two different things. When all you do is cater to someone else's needs a sense of self can easily be lost. Especially to a card-carrying member of the ME generation.

"But if I work at it, I think there are ways of turning these feelings around. It is going to be critical for me to keep finding ways to improve myself while caring for a child. Somehow a new accomplishment/reward cycle must be established—one very different from the one that used to drive us through college and grad school and up the career ladder. Yet it must be equally motivating and effective in fending off fears of loss of identity and self-esteem. We have to learn ways to validate ourselves in our own eyes without looking to others, or the system to do so.

"For one thing, there is no reason why personal and mental development cannot be far greater for those who stay at home than those who must spend all their time working at a job with a single focus. There is a world of reading to get through, special fields of knowledge to explore, art and music. Just because people who meet you at parties may close down their interest in you once you say you are at home with your children does not mean that you are dull. You might in fact be the best read person there, an expert on world affairs or economics or a closet Picasso. You can be the one to open a topic of conversation.

"There is also no reason to stop taking care of yourself—how you look, how you dress. Personal appearance and a sense of physical well-being are crucial to self-worth in my book.

"Of course, I may be deceiving myself about both the amount of free time I will have and how much energy and drive I will have to work at all these goals. But at least the goals are there."

* * * *

That is a fairly accurate look at an identity crisis from the inside but Eugenia has also begun to formulate an effective way to resolve it. She has faced up to the fact that she is not what she did, even though the crisis keeps on insisting that she is now going to be nothing more than a mom.

Being a mother is far from nothing. It is one of the most important careers in the world. That society does not accord it the status it deserves is society's fault. At the same time, being a mother does not define who you are. You are who you always were, and you can be who you want to grow to be.

Now it is time to look at another group who, as a class, seem to be afflicted with an identity crisis.

CHAPTER EIGHT
Senior Citizens and Self-Esteem

Happiness in the older years of life,
like happiness in every year of life, is
a matter of choice—your choice for yourself."

Harold Azine

IN HIS book, *Your Aging Parents* (Thomas More Press), John Deedy says:

> Let's open on a note of realism: Whatever the impressions that might be conveyed by beaming senior citizens boarding buses to Disneyland or teeing up on palm-lined Florida golf courses, aging is not a fun thing. Growing old translates to loss: loss of figure, of looks, of strength, of job, or close friends, of old enjoyments. Some people age like a good wine, and do great things with their old age. Goethe completed *Faust* at age 82; Luigi Cornaro at 95 demonstrated how Venice could reclaim its wasteland. But aging is not an exciting adventure for everyone. 'Getting old is pure hell,' remarks Ruth M. Snow of Baltimore, Maryland. 'Aging in itself strips you of your independence, which in turn results in losing your dignity, your self-esteem, and everything else. All you need to do is visit a nursing home or a home for the aged, and no other explanations are needed. I've seen them all, and indeed they are depressing.'

There have been and still are cultures that bestow a special dignity and status to their older members, but ours is not among them. Being old equates with being over the hill, out of it, lost in the twilight zone. Too often it also means being isolated, lonely and bored.

Aging brings plenty of physical and emotional problems. For the person who has identified who she or he is with the work or role played in life, it is doubly devastating, because he or she now feels stripped of self-identity and the esteem that attached itself to that

87

identity. Like the woman who leaves her career to care for children and assumes the generic identity of housewife, the retiree is stripped of uniqueness and becomes just another old person—or so too many perceive themselves to be.

The classic case of the retired man who doesn't know what to do with himself and mopes and prowls about the house, making his wife's life miserable is all too common. If she has been a housewife, at least in her latter years, she has probably learned to be at ease with her self-image and how to fill her life and find her satisfaction in a whole range of activities. But shorn of his job the retired man literally does not know what to do with all these empty hours of freedom because he doesn't know who he is or what he is supposed to be—and do. He may fish, play golf, build a cabinet but these are things he used to do as recreation. Now he cannot enjoy them on a full-time basis because he knows he is not a real golfer, a fisherman, or a cabinet-maker.

If an older couple have children they may still have an identity as mother or father, and derive some status and fulfillment from playing out the role of respected parent and doting grandparent. But our culture has conspired to make that prospect a very long shot indeed. Children are likely to be scattered across the country, either immersed in a frantic lifestyle and/or tied to a demanding work schedule which doles out stingy amounts of vacation time.

Older couples of means derive much satisfaction

Who Do You Think You Are?

from travel, from leisurely sightseeing tours, from visits to old friends and with their grown children. But this is really just another form of recreation which is a way of passing the time and keeping the question of identity and self-esteem at bay.

All of which is a shame, because in so many cases it really does not have to be this way. No one can fend off the debilitating onslaughts of the aging process or what it does to appearance and physical powers that we all take for granted—hearing, vision, dexterity. It is far better to accept these diminishments for what they are, fight them as much as possible but also realize that it is possible to work and live around them, rather than simply sit down in an easy chair and bemoan one's fate.

It may not be necessary to view things as dramatically as did poet Dylan Thomas when he wrote:

> Do not go gentle into that good night,
> Old age should burn and rave at close of day;
> Rage, rage against the dying of the light.

But it is vital that older people realize that they still have the same intrinsic self-worth that they have always laid claim to. The fact that society—even one's children—no longer validates you does not mean that your accomplishments, your accumulated wisdom, your veteran personality (honed to richness by years of interaction with all sorts of people), count as nothing. Nor is there anything wrong with relishing memories of past triumphs, or trying to recapture the echoes of love and passion. It is all the better if you have others to share these things with but if no one seems to appreciate you as they once did that is their loss.

Isolation and boredom are poor and often esteem-destroying companions. It is not always possible, especially in small towns and in rural settings, but older people—singles and couples alike—should make an effort to get out of the house or apartment.

In many communities there are centers designed to provide a wide range of activities—bridge, woodcarving, art classes, discussion groups, day and weekend bus tours and outings to plays, museums and concerts. They also offer counseling, help in finding apartments, medical care, assistance in negotiating the mazes of paperwork involved in social security, Medicare, federal and state taxes. They will gladly accept your services as a volunteer worker and some will even find you a full or part-time paying job.

Perhaps even more importantly, involvement with such a community center makes it easy to find and make new friends, people like you—friends who want to hear about your life and want you to take an interest in theirs.

Involvement with such a community center also puts you in touch with many civic and social systems and professionals. These can provide the sort of back-up, support and temporary care which may well make it possible for you to stay in your home through med-

Who Do You Think You Are?

ical or financial crises that might otherwise force you into a nursing home causing you to lose the last great bastion of self-identity—your independence. A broad range of esteem-restoring support systems may be waiting for you just around the corner or a brief bus ride away. Check your Yellow Pages; ask your neighbors.

At this point, I know there are some older readers who may be thinking, "This is all easy for you to say, but you have to be old to know what we're up against." And I am sure you are right. So let's hear from a ninety-year old man who, though wishing to remain anonymous, is quite willing to tell it like it is—and has been—for him.

First Person Singular

"When I first retired at 65 I didn't think of myself as old—just through with 38 years of civil, mechanical and architectural engineering. At 90, I do think of myself as old—I don't have much choice— but I no longer think of myself as retired. When you have been retired for 25 years you forget what it was like to be a member of the rat race.

"To me, getting old means having things taken away from you. First, and minor as it now seems, I took it hard when I had to give up driving. It is not that you cannot get around any more but that you have to depend on somebody else to haul you. And it sort of sums up or symbolizes all those little physical losses that have been coming on slowly—not seeing so well, reacting slower, getting confused by sudden traffic situations, and the like.

"Getting old also means—obviously—being a survivor. Some people just seem to survive more things than others. I've had a heart attack and two pacemaker implants. I survived a stroke and came back from that. I survived the shingles but that cost me most of my hearing—something very big taken away.

"All those hours in hospitals taught me patience. You have to learn to be something of a stoic if you live to my age. The way I see it you can endure suffering and confinement with bitterness or with resignation. Either way you suffer but at least you don't have to torment yourself or those who care for you by being bitter.

"Not that I haven't felt resentment. Once you reach a certain age younger people seem to stop seeing you as an individual. Except to those who love you, you simply don't count. It is hard to get jostled and shunted out of the way in crowds. I was captain of a university wrestling team and I can't help wishing I could have my strength back for just a minute in those situations.

"The young want everything to move fast. They let their impatience show in their eyes. Even my own children do this. When you are hard of hearing it is worse. People get impatient when you try to join in. They yell in your face. Finally they just give up on you and act like you are not there because it is too

Who Do You Think You Are?

much trouble to try and keep you in the flow of things. I guess because this disability came to me so late in life I have had more trouble adjusting to it—I am impatient with myself and have trouble accepting it. It embarrasses me not to know how loudly I'm talking. I have trouble shopping and ordering in restaurants. I keep thinking that my inability to hear is like a bruised muscle or a strained back—that it will go away one night and I'll be able to hear again.

"You asked me if I enjoy remembering things from the past. Well I do. I was born in 1898 and it is as if there are reels and reels of movies in my head, all starting at different times in different eras. I can go back and start one up any time. Different people, dressed differently, living in rooms and houses without electricity. And all starring a different me, of course. My wife and I, when we were first married, is a favorite. We spent two years living in various little houses—not much more than shacks, really—by roaring streams, putting the first paved roads through the Smoky Mountain National Park.

"So I get great pleasure from reliving the past but I don't ever want to get to the point where I am *living* in the past. The past—what I did and accomplished and endured and loved—are all part of who I am, but that "I" is all that I have left and it is in one way very little, and in another way very big. You get stripped of all pretensions and illusions about yourself at 90. So you have to learn to live with who you are. Maybe the single best thing about being old is that you really do not care so much what other people think about you.

"Life is a great gift in itself and you want to hang onto it, even when you cannot reasonably say to yourself, 'I will do such and such next year.' There may not be a next year, or even a tomorrow, but the human will to live and survive does not surrender to that sort of pessimism. I am happy with my life as it is. I am very fortunate because my wife is still with me. How it would be without her I don't even want to think about. We are blessed. We still live together on our own in an apartment.

I have to be honest. My biggest fear is not death, it is going into a nursing home. I am not sure I can handle that. I guess a lot of people feel the same way and they do have to go into one, and they survive, somehow. But at my age, I think the next health crisis is going to be the one that will take me right on out.

"The thing is, at least for me, that being institutionalized, no matter how well I might be treated, would take away the one last thing I cannot bear to part with—my sense of personal worth and independence. I just would not be me."

CHAPTER NINE
Picking Up the Pieces
Self-Esteem for the Widowed and Divorced

*"Hope is the feeling that you have
that the feeling you have isn't
permanent."*

Jean Kerr

THEY are always there on the application form. Two words and two little boxes: Married ☐ Single ☐. You must check one or the other and the one you check is an important part of your self-image.

At some point in our lives, all of us have checked the single box and to those who remain single, checking it is no big deal. (I do not mean to discount the pangs of regret or disappointment of those who wish desperately to find someone with whom to share their lives, or those whose love affairs may have turned sour.)

But to the married person who has lost a spouse through death, desertion or divorce, checking the single box can be a stinging reminder that she or he can no longer claim the double or united self-image that marriage bestows. As in the case of the doctor who responds automatically to the question of what she or he does with the words, "I am a doctor," rather than "I practice medicine," language exposes the real sense of self-image.

Ask a married woman (or man) what she has been doing lately, or where he is planning to go on vacation and you are likely to hear, "We have been fixing up the apartment," or "We are going to explore the west." Married people, for better or worse, tend to regard themselves as a unit, so much so that in happy marriages, the individual self seems to disappear, or at least dim itself. Folk wisdom has it that married couples even begin to look like one another.

However blissful this may appear to be, it is just as

much an illusion that personal self dies as it is that resemblances begin to merge (unconscious mimicking of personal mannerisms, body language and speech patterns create this effect). It is not a bad thing that in a working, enduring marriage this dual identity prevails, that individual selves defer to each other to the point where they seem to vanish.

It is, in fact, what makes for love—love of spouse and love of children. Good parents know that their children are not given them to fulfill their unmet needs or fantasies of achievement and celebrity. Love has never meant not having to say you are sorry; love is the willingness to give more than you get, the readiness to place one's self second. And, accepted on these terms, love, marriage and parenting can be among life's most rewarding and fulfilling experiences.

But as any widowed or divorced person can tell you, when, for whatever reason, this dual self-image is shattered, it makes for a wrenching adjustment.

The Naked Self

While the end result of divorce and widowhood are the same, and the personal pain is comparable, the events leading up to many divorces trigger a rebirth of the sense of single self which may help prepare the divorcee for the readjustment process.

It is the awareness of having been betrayed or rejected, of a growing realization that one's marriage partner is no longer willing to give as well as take,

Who Do You Think You Are?

or that he or she has fallen in love with someone else. The potential divorcee has—in many, though certainly not all cases—felt the resurgence of personal ego, if only in the sense that it is somehow being wronged or cheated. Anger and bitterness are powerful fuels for the resurgence of that sense of self. Once one says, "I'll show that creep that I can get along without him (her)," the I word, and the I identity are at least back in action.

The person whose beloved wife or husband dies may be slower to begin this adjustment, especially if they have been married for more than a year or two. There may have been some emotional preparation dictated by the harsh terms of a painful struggle against a terminal illness, but even then, the surviving spouse is reluctant to confront the reality of loss of the dual identity that has sustained him or her for so long.

In any case, the agony of grief and the terrible sense of emptiness settle in and a period of mourning must be lived through. One must pass through the painful but classic steps of human reaction to loss: denial that such a thing could happen; anger at God, fate, even the dead spouse, for daring to do such a thing; acute, smothering depression and numbness; and finally acceptance of the reality that I am no longer we, but only me.

This is a tough ordeal. It is especially difficult for the widow and homemaker who has always thought of herself only as her husband's wife and/or their children's mother. In effect, her sense of self has been reborn after years of submersion in her dual identity. This can be as true for strong, successful, socially prominent women as it is for their more ordinary sisters.

In her autobiography, *Kitty*, Kitty Carlisle, chairman of the New York State Council on the Arts, tells of the trauma she experienced when her husband, the famous playwright Moss Hart died in 1961. She was suddenly left alone, financially well fixed, but with two children, ages 11 and 13, to raise.

"I didn't know how to make a life," she confesses. "I thought of suicide." But she finally pulled herself out of the black hole of her long depression with the help of her husband's philosophy: "You don't escape from life, you escape *into* it."

Rebuilding Single Self-Image

Moss Hart's insight—"You don't escape from life, you escape into it"—are words for every widowed and divorced person to remember and act upon. The pain of separation may persist for a long time but sooner or later you must face up to the reality of both your loss and your new single self-identity. If you feel overwhelmed by the long list of things you have to learn about, such as managing money, taking care of a car, filing state and federal income taxes, do not give into the feeling of hopelessness and wallow in self-pity, get out there and meet those challenges.

Who Do You Think You Are?

You will find the motivation by considering the alternatives—a lifetime of the same self-pity and perhaps a grim financial and social future. (And isn't it strange, that just when you need old friends and familiar settings the most, they seem to evaporate. People who knew you as "us" seem to feel strange and uneasy when they meet one-to-one with just plain you. Your grief may alarm and threaten them. They do not want to offend either you or your ex by seeming to play favorites. They worry that traditional parties and occasions may remind you of your late spouse and cause you pain. Whatever. Add them all up and they total virtually zero.)

You will find the method and the path through this overwhelming task of learning and doing by breaking it down into bite-size pieces, by making lists, by setting priorities (I have to get the car in good working order and keep it that way in order to have the necessary mobility to apply for a job), by asking for both advice and help (people love to give advice and if you listen to it and marvel at its wisdom you will so charm the advisor that he or she may actually provide concrete help). Do not be afraid to expose either your ignorance or your need to people you have reason to trust. The main thing is to get moving.

If that is the main thing, the best thing is that just moving forward will make a positive difference almost at once. It certainly did for an acquaintance. Kaye's husband of 24 years died of a massive and totally unexpected heart attack at age 50; Kaye was 48. They had one son who was a sophomore in college at the time. This is how it went for her.

First Person Singular

"When Ken died suddenly four years ago my first reaction was simply not to believe it. I mean, I knew it was a fact that he was gone but another part of my head or heart refused to accept it. When the fact finally sank in I turned bitter and self-pitying. How could he have done this to me? How could God do this to me? How on earth am I going to manage?

"After the funeral and the burial I went back home and went to bed. I never wanted to get up again. When I finally did get up, I went around the house in a daze. I was so far down I was numb. I did not feel whole. I felt Ken was still there even though I couldn't see him or touch him. I have read stories about soldiers who have lost a leg or an arm in battle. They still feel aches and pains in the missing knee or elbow.

"There was a terrible quiet, an aching empty space. I never knew what loneliness was until then. I had spent many days by myself over the years of marriage but I was never lonely because Ken would be coming home.

"I was not the weepy type but I must have been as depressing to be around as I was depressed. Many of our old friends invited me over, or dropped by during the day but I did not respond nor did I make them feel welcome. Yet, when they finally quit trying to console me and cheer me up I resented it. I remember thinking that it probably was not me they liked but Ken, who was witty and outgoing. Just plain old me couldn't attract anything but flies.

"Finally reality began to force its way into my life in the form of money. When the lawyers and the tax people got things sorted out I had the house but we had bought it just five years before Ken died and it took most of the insurance and some of our modest savings to pay it off. Our son Tom offered to drop out of college but neither he nor I really wanted that. If I sold the house and found an apartment he would be able to finish school. If I could find an entry level job somewhere I would be able to live fairly comfortably—at least for ten years or so, barring rampant inflation.

"I was not thrilled by the prospect of having to sell our (I was still thinking in the plural in those days) beautiful new house nor by the challenge of finding a job, but at least I had something to do. Selling the house was not difficult and after I had moved into a bright new apartment I began, at last, to think of it as my place. But I still found other ways I missed Ken. I had never done anything with the car except get in and drive it. Now there was the business of getting the oil and filter changed, getting state and city tags on time and in place, seeing that the insurance was renewed.

"Thank goodness that Ken had always insisted that

Joel Wells

I manage the checking account. He had also engaged me—against my will at first—in managing our small investments and in filling out the income tax forms. Not that I could really do all the taxes involved in settling Ken's estate and selling the house but at least I knew enough to get the right kind of help. Being in an apartment spared me from all the maintenance and yard work the house had entailed and I was thankful for that.

"Rating my employment qualifications was humbling. I had a college degree in American literature and I could type, but I doubted that either of those achievements would count for much in the computer era. Then there was my age and appearance. All of a sudden I was self-conscious about both. Did anyone want a plumpish 48-year-old woman as a secretary or a receptionist? I doubted it. And clothes? How should I dress when I went for job interviews? By the time I forced myself to go to an employment agency I had about as much confidence and self-esteem as a boiled potato. And it showed.

I got a job all right, filing and typing and answering the phone in the cramped little offices of an alcoholic dentist. He was totally disorganized, constantly missing or cancelling appointments and badly in need of somebody to blame for his failing practice—namely, me. And, fool that I was, I took all his abuse and criticism to heart, believing that if I really was a capable worker I could have gotten everything straightened out. He finally drove me to tears and I walked out and never went back.

"That was my low point but it was also a turning point. I went home wallowing in self-pity, drank a couple of glasses of wine and on an impulse called a woman who had been one of my closest friends in college. She listened to my tale of woe for a few minutes and then, almost rudely, told me to shut up and listen to her. She was a guidance counselor for a social services agency. And she assured me that there was nothing unique about my situation. She said that the only person who could change my life was me. And the me she remembered in college had been a bright, ambitious, capable and attractive person with a lot to offer the world. Now because I had lost a lot— and losing your husband is a huge loss—I was thinking and acting like I had lost everything, including the self I was before I married. She made me promise to visit her at her office the next day. Then she asked me something utterly preposterous: 'Are you a baseball fan?' I told her, 'No.' 'That's a shame,' she said, 'because if you were, you would know that you will never get to second base until you take your foot off first.'

"And that is exactly what my friend made it possible for me to do. With great difficulty I forced myself to take my foot off the base of a past life that had been a great one, but which was over. I took the first step by going to see her, and after that I just kept on going.

Joel Wells

"Not that any overnight miracles took place—it took more nerve than I thought I had, and more persistence. My friend suggested that before I looked for another job that I work in her social agency as a volunteer for a few months. I enjoyed working with people. I learned how computers work. I got the right clothes and took an interest in my appearance. I shed twenty pounds and began to feel better about myself. I kept so busy that I no longer had much time to dwell on the past and the things that might have been. I made new friends who shared my new interests. I introduced my new friends to some of the old ones and they get along well.

"A vacancy appeared on the agency's staff and the job was offered to me. Not only did it pay a decent salary but it provided medical coverage and a pension. Tom graduated from college and found a good job with an engineering firm. He's married now and I am going to be a grandmother in a couple of months.

"Do I still miss Ken?

"You bet I do!

"Can I live without him?

"You bet I can!"

CHAPTER TEN
An Overview

*"It is better to know some of the
questions than all of the answers."*

James Thurber

BEFORE we look at ways to renew and bolster self-esteem let us review some major themes.

We all have a real self which is comprised of some basic realities and universal human traits. The real self is hard to define and harder still for us to visualize because it is difficult to stand back and see ourselves. As philosopher Allan Watts says, "Trying to define yourself is like trying to bite your own teeth."

In Chapter Four a rough formula for expressing it was nonetheless set down. The real self is that in us which says: "I am alive; I like myself because of who I am; I want to grow, learn, experience fulfillment, and be happy."

The real self is highly susceptible to both praise and criticism. A life-long process of comparison and measurement begins. This results in the building of a self-image that embraces the real person and the results of those comparisons and measurements which we accept as the truth about ourselves whether or not they actually reflect reality.

These measurements and comparisons can sometimes be positive and enhance or inflate our self-image. They are more often negative, since our culture has a way of holding up perfection images that are impossible to achieve while at the same time teaching us to equate lack of perfection with total failure.

These destructive comparisons we have called put-downs, some of which we simply receive by living, observing and listening, especially in our younger and adolescent years. Other put-downs are laid on us deliberately by thoughtless and even malicious people who may be diverting attention from their own insecurities. Then there are what we call self put-downs, failings we charge ourselves with because of false expectations, negative thinking, and the fact that we let one failure or painful experience from the past condition us to believe that we will continue to fail.

There is no avoiding the construction of a self-image. It is neither good nor bad in itself. It is a complex and pervasive conception made up of a number of recognizable components, including body or physical self-image, as well as intellectual, social, psychological and sexual self-images.

Another component of self-image is role-identity. The distinction may be difficult to grasp since the terms seem so closely related as to appear redundant. As we saw, however, people tend to equate who they are with what they do. This is an artificial notion but a potent one. It allows professional and social norms to dictate personal esteem as contemporary fads and fashions change. It relegates certain people to a sort of low-status dustbin—housewives and mothers who devote their lives to raising a family, retirees and older people, widows, the unemployed and those on welfare, etc.

It is only when this total self-image becomes distorted, needlessly negative, and badly out of tune with reality that it becomes destructive and smothers the real self. Without some measure of self-esteem, self-confidence, self-love, and a viable self-identity we risk entering deep and prolonged depression and self-destructive behavior.

Everyone has a real self that justifies affirming. Nobody is worthless.

CHAPTER ELEVEN
Assessing Your Self-Image

*Your vision will become clear only
when you look into your own heart. . . .
Who looks outside, dreams; who looks
inside, awakes.''*

Carl Jung

THE title of this book asks the question, "Who do you think you are?" And it is the question that this brief chapter invites you to examine. I am simply going to ask you to look inside yourself, as psychiatrist Carl Jung prescribes, and give honest responses to a series of queries. Some of them may not apply to you, most will.

The purpose of the exercise is not to make you feel good or bad about yourself, but simply to help you get a clearer idea of your own self-image by thinking about things most of us seldom confront in a formal or conscious way.

There are no right or wrong answers but, if you wish, you may find it illuminating to decide whether your answers are on the positive or negative side of the scale of self-esteem with the notation "P" or "N."

Were you a happy child?

Did your parents make you feel loved?

Did they make you feel special?

Did you get along with other children—brothers, sisters, cousins, playmates?

Was there anything you hated about yourself?

Was there anything that you were ashamed of about your body or appearance?

Did other children make fun of you?

Did they bully you in school?

Joel Wells

Were you a bully?

Did you like elementary school?

Hate it?

Did you have any subject at which you excelled?

At which you failed?

Were you good at sports?

Just so-so?

Terrible?

When you were in high school were you popular?

Did you have a close group of friends?

A best friend of the same sex?

Did you enjoy school social activities?

Were you involved in extra-curricular activities—
clubs, newspaper, year book, cheer leading, band?

Were you on any of the school's athletic teams?

Did you hate gym classes?

Did you feel self-conscious or ashamed in communal
school showers?

Were you proud of your body?

Not proud but not ashamed of it?

Who Do You Think You Are?

Despised it?

Were you an honors student?

An average student?

Just trying to get by?

Did you go to school dances, proms, etc.?

Did you date a lot?

Did you have a steady?

Did you feel left out or persecuted by your fellow students?

Did you plan right along to go to college?

Did you want to go to college if it turned out to be possible?

Had no interest in going?

Did you feel comfortable taking friends home with you to see your parents and where you lived?

Or were you uncomfortable about this?

As a young adult were you excited about the future?

Do you feel you can handle just about any social or personal situation you find yourself in?

Or are there some situations and challenges which you try to avoid because you know you can not cope well with?

117

Joel Wells

Are you confident about the way you dress?

Do you feel that your vocabulary and grasp of good grammar are superior?

Or do you sometimes keep quiet for fear of exposing your shortcomings in these areas?

If you are not married or romantically involved with someone, do you wish you were?

Is there some reason, other than just waiting for the right person to come along, that you are not so attached?

What is it?

Do you like your job or profession?

Do you just tolerate it?

Do you despise it?

Do you feel that you have gone as far as you can go at work?

If so, are you planning to move on?

Do you consider yourself happily married?

Do you think of yourself as a good lover?

Do you think your partner regards you as a good lover?

Are you a good and capable parent?

Who Do You Think You Are?

Or do your kids baffle, frustrate and disobey you more often than they do not?

Are you happy as a mother and homemaker or would you like to have a job or career as well?

What would you change about your appearance if you could?

Do you think you make a favorable first impression on people you meet?

Do you think you are an interesting conversationalist?

Do you think you have a good sense of humor?

Are you afraid to tell jokes or make a verbal display of wit?

Do you have a friend, or friends, with whom you discuss personal problems and share your hopes and fears?

Or are you a loner in this respect, believing that any such revelations are a sign of weakness?

Do you ever open up to anyone—including your spouse or lover?

Do you handle money wisely or do budgets and check books throw you for a loop?

How are you at problem handling, keeping schedules, coping with unexpected crises?

Do you thrive on a big work load and lots of details to deal with?

Are you a confident motorist or does heavy traffic frighten you?

Do you enjoy travel or would you rather stay close to home?

Do you have trouble handling criticism and sarcasm directed at you?

Do you feel threatened about losing your temper?

Would you rate yourself as an assertive type, ready, willing and able to speak up and stand up for your rights even if it means a hostile confrontation?

Or do you feel more comfortable either giving in to another person's assertiveness, rudeness, thoughtlessness, selfishness or aggression so long as the situation goes away?

Do you honestly feel that you are basically a moral person who can be counted on to do the right thing and respect the rights of others?

Have you ever done anything of which you are deeply ashamed?

Do you consider yourself physically fit—at least for your age and lifestyle?

Or have you given up on your appearance and health?

Do you look forward to each new day or do you dread it?

Who Do You Think You Are?

Do you plan ahead for vacations, special trips, outings, visits to family and friends?

Do you buy yourself special presents?

Do you have hobbies, a favored form of recreation (other than television)?

Is there something you are particularly good at and in which you take special pride?

Do you ever wish that you were somebody else?

Overall, if such a radical simplification could be made, do you consider yourself a winner or a loser in the game of life?

There are many more questions which could be asked, of course. Perhaps some of those listed here will suggest others more meaningful to you. The answers do not define the totality of your self-image but they will serve as a rough outline of it which will be useful as we now turn to the business of updating and what, for want of a better word, we will call housecleaning that self-image.

CHAPTER TWELVE
Updating Your Self-Image

*"We only become what we are
by the radical and deep-seated
refusal of that which others have
made of us."*

Jean-Paul Sartre

SINCE your ultimate goal is to get back in touch with real self and, as noted in the Introduction, that jewel may be lost somewhere in the attic of our minds, it is necessary to throw out a lot of junky components of self-image in order to get at it.

That menal housecleaning is step one. Step two is to update your self-image so that it more accurately conforms with the present reality of your life. This is accomplished by making some conscious adjustments to some subconscious assumptions and to some old sore spots that may no longer prove so sensitive when you actually reach back and touch them.

Step three entails adjusting outdated or unrealistic self-expectations you still cling to in spite of the fact that they are either hopelessly out of reach or are worthless, artificial and unimportant.

Step four involves sorting out the unrealistic expectations which we have received from others and which we have allowed to dictate the terms of our self-esteem.

And finally we will take a look at something I call alternative thinking which incorporates both a negative and a positive side. It is an approach that is useful in freeing one from old hang-ups.

Housecleaning

In the assessment questions listed in Chapter Eleven did you notice that there were a disproportionate number dealing with childhood and adolescence? Perhaps not so disproportionate when you consider how much of our self-image is formed in the early years of life. It is during those years that we are most vulnerable to put-downs, when we have not had a sufficiently broad experience of the world and people to put them in perspective, to realize that no one is perfect, or to have grown a thicker, less sensitive skin.

Skin is a useful metaphor here. It is a fact that, like snakes, we shed and regrow our skins over and over in a lifetime—we just do not do it all at once. Yet we hang onto those barbs and negative comparisons that get under our youthful skins for years. Teeth are another useful simile: we lose all our baby teeth but we refuse to give up our baby put-downs.

Does it really matter to the person you are today that mommy seemed to like your brother better than she did you?

How does it affect you as an adult that you are a bit shorter than normal—whatever normal is?

Why should it still bother you that high school kids laughed at you in the shower room?

So you had a tough time learning math. Does it still make you feel you are stupid, given all the things you have mastered and accomplished?

It is possible to put most of the self-image assessment questions which bear on childhood and adolescence to this test. Do it to them, one at a time. Gather up those that no longer bother you or seem relevant and toss them into some strongly imaged receptacle— a trash compacter or, better yet, a garbage disposal.

Who Do You Think You Are?

But wait. Before you turn on the switch and grind up these obsolete chunks of negative self-image up, be sure you have included all the counterproductive associations attached to them. Okay, so you are no longer worried about all the problems with learning you had in grade school, but it is no good scrapping that nagging, useless memory unless you also scrap your continuing fear and reluctance to approach seemingly complex new problems and ideas. Force yourself to realize that it was the original self put-down about being stupid in grade school which is the direct cause of your self-limiting behavior in the present. If you have no problem getting rid of the cause, why hang onto the effect?

Yes, this is definitely easier said than done. It does not follow that you cannot do it. When the next such mental challenge confronts you the same old mental choke-up syndrome will try to take charge and shut down your confidence. But instead of letting your pre-programmed emotions fog up your vision and reason, step back a moment, take a deep breath and remind yourself that this is not the way it has to be. There is no reason in the world why you should be afraid or doubt your ability to tackle this challenge. You got rid of that hang-up, remember. Now take up the challenge again in the businesslike fashion with which you undertake everything else. Don't try to swallow it all at once, to absorb it via some cosmic flash of intuition. Hard problems are solved in steps. Simply take the first one. If you persist, you will be pleasantly surprised at the results.

All right, start your disposal.

Adjusting Your Self-Image

Housecleaning can accomplish wonders, but it is no substitute for redecorating. Some things cannot be easily disposed of. There are still going to be tacky and tarnished blocks of self-image to deal with. If you are still convinced that you are basically unattractive, for instance—a conviction that you accepted in your youth and which time has done nothing to dispel—must you live with it? Perhaps, but how much does it really matter to you on a day-to-day basis? Need you carry its weight around with you like a shopping bag full of bricks? It would be a lot more comfortable and reasonable to stash the bag in some back closet of your mind and get on with the good things in life.

It is possible to make such adjustments in your self-image. It takes some practice and requires desensitizing your self-consciousness. Your looks are far more important to you than they are to other people. They may have—in your eyes—blighted your romantic life. They may have, in fact, caused you to become a self-fulfilling prophecy: because you felt unattractive you present yourself as unappealing; you exude unattractiveness in your posture, your approach to people, your speech, your invisible but very real negative signals that you do not think much of yourself, so why

Who Do You Think You Are?

should others. If you were a plump, short-sighted boy, you may well have grown into a fat, bespectacled man—and now bald, to boot.

Unless some mad chemist finally comes up with a potion that will really grow hair (and not just fuzz, as the latest compound to hit the market does), you are stuck with being bald or going the toupee route. However, you can get contact lenses or some less klutzy frames for your trifocals. If you are strongly enough motivated you can lose that extra weight.

These are adjustments to your physical self-image which may spur you to make some adjustments to your psychological self-image. You may or may not realize the romantic fulfillment you long for but you can desensitize that constant feeling of unattractiveness by realizing that if you put that monkey on the back burner and stop acting like a wimp, you will soon stop feeling like one and, wonder of wonders, other people will like and accept you just the way you are.

Most of us have experienced the phenomenon that proves this true. It happens everywhere people are thrown together for a period of time—in the military service, in offices, on prolonged travel tours. At first meeting or gathering you instinctively attach labels to others based primarily on external appearance. She is the fat lady; he is the ugly guy. There may be a string bean, a baldy, a pock face, a shorty and a loud-mouth. But after a few days or weeks these people have a marvelous way of turning into Wanda, George, Pete,

Martha, Tom, Nancy—accepted individuals now, not just labels. All but loud mouth, whom you still think of as a label, not because of the way he looks but because his over-inflated self-image as a superior observer and expert on human nature drive him to live out his role every minute of every day.

Becoming less sensitive, less self-conscious is the key to blunting the destructive effects of the low self-esteem that cannot otherwise be dealt with. It is only necessary to realize that these perceived shortcomings and lacks of perfection are of little importance or concern to others—providing you do not let them shape and control your behavior so as to constantly call attention to them. There is wisdom in writer Fran Lebowitz's adage: "All God's children are not beautiful. Most of God's children are, in fact, barely presentable."

Adjusting Expectations

If I recall correctly, financier Bernard Baruch once boasted that by the time he was 30 he had a million dollars for each year of his age. For Mr. Baruch, who did not suffer from low self-esteem, it was evidently no more than he expected.

All of us have expectations in life. Many rise out of childhood and adolescent dreams and hopes.

"I am going to be a surgeon."

"I am going to be a great novelist."

"I am going to be a model."

Who Do You Think You Are?

"I am going to be a rock star."

"I am going to be a professional golfer."

"I am going to be rich and famous."

These expectations usually fade away in the course of years and in the face of life as it is dealt to us. A few do become just what they intended to be but most of us shed these early expectations without a great sense of loss. The boy who would be a golf pro may still fantasize a bit as he watches the Open on television, but he manages to enjoy his Saturday morning duffer's game without putting himself down after each missed putt. The girl who dreamed of becoming a model can still take pride and pleasure from her carriage and appearance without turning green with envy every time she picks up a fashion magazine.

But there are other, more general but deeply rooted expectations that we harbor and cherish all our lives. These are more like unconditional demands we make on life—and on ourselves. When we fail to realize them we blame both life and ourselves. That is, we suffer both a keen sense of deprivation and a deep loss of self-esteem that may stay with us all our life.

This is tragic and it does not have to be. The truth is that expectations are hopes—wishes. And hopes and wishes, while they may come true, are not therefore bound to. The problem is that there are things we want so much, or things that we assume must be both true and forthcoming in our lives, that we feel cheated and diminished when they do not come to pass.

When they do not come our way, when things do not turn out as expected, we are hurt, baffled and unhappy with ourselves. The most common instance of this phenomenon is the marriage that breaks up because each partner enters it with a whole set of unformulated but nonetheless very powerful expectations both of what they want from the other spouse and from the marriage itself. Very often these are completely unrealistic expectations. Some people want mothering or fathering; others think they will be living out the pages of a long romantic novel. There are those who think all money problems will disappear, all loneliness, all strife and turmoil, all the cares of the world will vanish. Men believe that marriage will automatically make them settle down; women sometimes think that they can transform and remake a surly, unreliable male into a model husband and father. New parents are full of impossible expectations both for their children and for themselves in terms of what their children will bring to them in terms of pride, adoring love and fulfillment.

What I am getting at here is that another way to clear the needless clutter from our self-image is to take a close, hard look at some of the expectations you have carried around with you for so long. Why should something that was always just a possibility continue to make you feel badly about yourself and your life because it has not turned into a reality?

Granted, some expectations are more reasonable than others. It is reasonable to expect at least some happiness and love in marriage. It is reasonable for married people to think they can have children. It is reasonable to expect that those children will be happy, healthy and return your love. It is reasonable but it is not written in stone. Marriages turn bitter, some people are infertile, children are born with mental and physical disabilities. All of these things hurt and hurt badly. But they should not therefore diminish your worth or self-esteem.

There are many other expectations which may have been reasonable at one time (though never certainties) but which now, if you are honest with yourself, seem so unlikely that they should be put into your mental garbage disposal along with those early put-downs. And remember to include the negative associations and behaviors to which they are tied.

It is high time, for instance, for the middle-aged woman who has long since learned to manage a perfectly stable and otherwise happy single life and career, to stop letting her self-esteem be blighted because she has not found a husband. Just as it is time for the man who always expected to be moved into the top management echelons of his company, but who has been repeatedly passed over, to stop berating his incompetence and either enjoy the job he has or take another.

Most of us carry these obsolete expectations about with us long after we need to. There is nothing wrong with dreaming or reaching for the stars, but it is wrong to keep on punishing the dreamer when the dream fails to come true, or to cut off the arms of the star-reacher because they proved too short.

Dealing With Imposed Expectations

Another root cause of low self-esteem that can and should be examined in adulthood are the expectations which are imposed on us by others. Many of these are unnecessary and unrealistic but we have accepted them either consciously or unconsciously and when we fail to live up to them, we put ourselves down.

By expectations I mean not only goals but rules and limits of personal behavior. By others I mean not just parents, relatives, friends, but our ethnic background, culture, jobs, careers and institutions—even religion.

Neither parents nor first-born son really expect the lad to grow up and be president. But there is a whole range of parental expectations that are laid on most of us, some of which are quite reasonable, such as telling the truth, learning to share and be thoughtful of the needs and rights of others, making a sustained effort in school, and the like. But there are just as many other expectations, such as being the brightest, being first in everything, being a star athlete, never getting into trouble, taking parents as the ultimate role models, accepting their religious, political and world views as our own, etc., which are not realistic.

Living up to parental and family expectations has made thousands of lives miserable. Men and women find themselves in jobs and vocations they hate—and hate themselves for clinging to. People put themselves through misery and boredom following family routines and rituals. Many drag themselves off to church or temple to please the family or to meet the expectations of the community in spite of the fact that they have no real religious commitment. And in so doing, they saddle themselves with the self-image of conformist or hypocrite.

Cultural and family expectations have driven other thousands into marriages they only endure, and into potential roles they did not want or were not equipped to deal with. Syndicated columnist Ann Landers conducted two readership polls which dramatize this unhappy fact. Over 50,000 readers responded to her question: "If you had it to do over again, would you marry the person to whom you are now married?"

There were two sets of responses—those who signed their answers and those who did not. Seventy percent of those who signed, said yes; 30 percent, no. Of those who did not sign their responses, only 48 percent said yes and a whopping 52 percent said no.

In an earlier survey she asked readers to answer the question, "If you had it to do over again, would you have children?" The response, which Ann Landers called "staggering" and "disturbing" resulted in 70 percent answering no.

These statistics reveal the more serious consequences of accepting and living out the unrealistic expectations of others. There are other less harmful expectations but which nonetheless influence our atti-

Joel Wells

tudes, behavior and ultimately our self-esteem if and when we fail to observe them and sometimes when we do. Think of the things that lurk under such umbrella dictates as, "Nice girls don't...." "Big boys don't...." And there are almost universal expectations that one must always be polite on the telephone and that one is obliged to answer questions, especially personal questions. The whole telephone sales business thrives on the first of those assumptions, and reporters, poll-takers, product researchers and con men live by the second. The only time you *have* to answer questions is when you are on trial in a court of law. None of your business are four words that the world needs now.

There is certainly need for honesty and civility, there is an innate desire to please those who care about us. But the plain truth is that you do not have to do what others expect you to do. There may be negative consequences when those others have power over your life or job. I am not advocating that you become a rebel without a cause but most of us can raise our self-esteem and get closer to our real selves if we sort out and dispose of the many outdated and unrealistic expectations that others have imposed on us over the years. The more of these you shed the more completely you are your own person.

Alternative Thinking

In the process of trying to live up to our own expectations and those of others we tend to fall into thought and behavior patterns that are habitual. Whether we have failed at something or succeeded, we program ourselves to repeat the process or behavior even though there may be other and better ways to deal with the matter.

This example is not too savory, and not directly to the point because it is partly a physical problem, but due to a temperamental esophagus and an almost chronic sinus condition I used to be troubled with gagging, especially on cold winter mornings. For a while it got to the point where, even when I felt fine, if I so much as thought about it while walking to work I would start to gag. It became a source of embarrassment when people stopped and stared at me or offered assistance. It became even more so when I would go to the dentist's office before work and disrupt the place by gagging when he tried to put instruments or X-ray film holders in my mouth.

It finally dawned on me that the problem was more psychological than real. I convinced myself that covering my mouth with a scarf on cold mornings would stop the gagging—and after a while it did. I also realized that it only happened in the morning, so I scheduled my dental appointments in the afternoons and have not had a problem since, much to the relief of my dentist.

A new or alternative approach helped solve this negative and embarrassing self-expectation. The same approach can be useful in dealing with expectations of others that pose problems and threaten our self-esteem.

Joel Wells

In the movie, *Raiders of the Lost Ark*, there is a memorable scene in which our hero, Indiana Jones, carrying his trademark bull whip, is running through an Arab marketplace pursued and pursuing at the same time. Suddenly he is confronted by a huge man flourishing a wickedly curved scimitar. There is no escape route for Indiana. It is the movie audience's expectation, and certainly that of the swordsman, that Indiana is going to have to take him on with whip and fist. It is the expectation of the villain, made crystal clear by the sneer of anticipation of his face, that he is going to make mincemeat out of Indiana. Indiana himself seems to expect the worst. But then his face brightens as he remembers he has a splendidly effective alternative at his command. He pulls a revolver out of his belt and disposes of his sneering menace.

Closer to home and real life, I recently watched a toddler trying to deal with a new educational toy his mother sat before him. She carefully demonstrated how a series of cubes, balls and plastic squares should be inserted into a covered container only by matching the slots with corresponding shapes. When the toddler tried it on his own he met with no success and grew increasingly frustrated. He was not meeting his mother's expectations. He watched as she again matched things up and then removed the shapes from their container and turned them back over to him. Suddenly his little face lit up remarkably like Indiana Jones' did. He pulled the lid off the container and quickly threw in all the pesky shapes. As far as he was concerned he had solved the problem and met his mother's expectation.

There may not always be an alternative approach to difficult expectations but it is surprising what turning things around or inside out can often accomplish. Give it a try. Whether you use this technique to meet a challenging expectation or to eliminate a negative one, it can do wonders for your self-esteem.

CHAPTER THIRTEEN
Strengthening Your Self-Esteem

*"Do you know what happens to
scar tissue? It's the strongest
part of the skin."*

Michael Mantell

HAVING read this far your understanding and appreciation of yourself should already be enhanced. If you have disposed of obsolete and adolescent put-downs, refocused your sense of self-image, not on what you do but on who you are and adjusted your expectations to embrace only those that are authentically yours—you should be much closer to your real self.

But even in this more streamlined and realistic self-image there may be things you do not feel comfortable with, things that you wish were different, things that still undermine your self-esteem. So the problem remains that it is not always enough to know your real self, you must also accept and value it.

Unfortunately there is no magic formula for achieving this in a single bound. There is no handy phone booth to slip into, as mild-mannered Clark Kent does when he wants to turn himself into Superman. There are, however, several approaches or processes which psychologists and psychiatrists employ or recommend. There are many variations on these approaches but they boil down to learning how to accept yourself, warts and all, before you can begin to build true self-esteem.

Self-Acceptance

Alert readers will recall that the last Chapter said that there was a negative as well as a positive side to the technique of alternative thinking, but only positive examples were given. Perhaps the term negative is misleading, but the flip side to alternative thinking involves changing one's usual attitude from that of intense concern to that of convincing yourself that it (your problem, shortcoming, lack of perfection, etc.) does not really matter a great deal.

It is an approach that is best summed up by Dr. Elizabeth Kubler-Ross's maxim for self-acceptance: "I'm not okay, you're not okay, but that's okay."

There is certainly merit and a good deal of realism in this. If our goal is to achieve a calmness, an inner tranquility that lets us enjoy peace of mind and life to its fullest under the conditions that prevail for us— not for others more fortunate, gifted, or beautiful than ourselves—then this sort of total acceptance can work wonders.

"I know quadriplegics who can say, 'Fine,' when asked 'How are you?' " says Doctor Bernie Siegel in his book *Love, Medicine and Miracles.* He adds that it is "because they have learned to love and give themselves to the world. They are not denying their physical limits but rather transcending them."

This is admirable, but I think it is difficult for most people to keep that sense of loving and giving, that selfless mindset, in place for very long. For most of us, self is what we are and why we are living. It is one thing to accept it, it is another thing to give it up. What we are after is a deeper appreciation of it, one based on realities, the facts and conditions of our lives, not the unreal perceptions and expectations of ourselves or others.

Who Do You Think You Are?

To this end, it may be useful to employ another type of alternative thinking to arrive at a self-acceptance that may stay with us and fit more comfortably. Someone who always wanted to be married and have a family, for instance, may be able to better accept the fact she or he will not realistically realize those expectations by looking at the other side of their situation. Take off the rose-colored glasses through which you have too long idealized the romance of marriage and the rewards of child-rearing. Yes, you have missed something, but you have also been spared something—the something that prompted so many of Ann Landers' readers to confess that if they had it to do over, they would not have married the person they did, or have the children they had. Even at its best, marriage and family life can be hectic, constricting, frustrating, and time-consuming, so much so, that there is little left over to devote to your own potential and fulfillment. Contrast all this with the personal freedom and emotional independence which you have enjoyed and you will be happier about your singleness—and yourself.

There are many other instances where this sort of alternative thinking can be applied. It is not so much that all clouds have a silver lining, because they don't. But who you are and what your situation is may not be nearly as gloomy as you think when compared with who and what you think you would rather be. You may not be entirely happy with the reality but you can accept it as such. You are no longer wearing yourself out chasing empty dreams.

Joel Wells

In *Honoring the Self,* Dr. Nathaniel Brandon sums it up best: "If I can accept that I am who I am, that I feel what I feel, that I have done what I have done—if I can accept it whether I like it all or not—then I can accept my self-doubts, my poor self-esteem. And when I can accept all that, I have put myself on the side of reality rather than attempting to fight reality. I am no longer twisting my consciousness in knots to maintain delusions about my present condition. And so I clear the road for the first steps of strengthening my self-esteem."

Building Self-Esteem

Suppose your long lost fairy godmother showed up today and gave you three wishes. Three-wish jokes abound because the butts of them fail to think about the consequences of their wishes. So be careful.

Let's say you wished to be tall, dark and handsome instead of being like me—medium height, balding, and a bit overweight. Zappo—you suddenly bear a striking resemblance to actor Tom Selleck. You rush to look in the mirror and fail to recognize yourself. Your clothes no longer fit. You like the way you look but you still feel the same inside. Then your wife comes into the room, screams and runs to the phone to call the police about the home invader; your children come home from school and they scream—but only because they want Tom Selleck's autograph.

Who Do You Think You Are?

Sure, girls you pass on the street stare and go ga-ga, but your friends won't recognize you.

However, you are still too pleased with your physical transformation to sort things out. So you ask your FGM for a fancy red sports car to run around town in. There it is in the driveway. One small problem presents itself—you can't drive a stick shift and you have a fender bender at the first intersection. The police come and of course you don't have a title for the car (FGMs are notoriously inept about paperwork) and your description and driver's license photo don't look a thing like the person who drove his red Porsche through a stop sign. So it's off to jail. Your lawyer will not bail you out because he doesn't recognize you—and of course neither does your wife. Things look so hopelessly complicated that in desperation you say to yourself, "Why did I ever get into this mess? I wish I was my old self again."

And before you can say "Magnum," you are. And, in spite of the fact that the Porsche went back into Never-Never Land at the same time, you are very, very happy.

The moral of this little parable is that you are who you are. There's nothing wrong with wanting to be an improved you, or a happier you, but for better or worse you cannot be anyone other than you.

So why not appreciate and esteem and celebrate the you you are?

Begin by asking yourself what's not to like.

Joel Wells

Okay, there are things you are not happy with. Can any of them be changed? Yes, you can lose weight, quit smoking, get into shape, get some decent clothes, go to an assertiveness course, get your teeth capped, have plastic surgery, improve your vocabulary, learn new job skills, join some social clubs, get out and meet people and buy a toupee. And, if you can resummon your courage and determination, you can get out of a destructive marriage or relationship; you can quit your nowhere job; you can move out of your depressing apartment or your menacing neighborhood; you can enroll in an adult education course or attend a trade school or join the army.

But while you can definitely make yourself more attractive, you cannot make yourself handsome or beautiful. You cannot make yourself taller or shorter. You cannot change your voice, or suddenly grow gorgeous curves. If you are handicapped it is likely that you will remain so. You are not likely (short of winning the lottery) to become rich. So what?

The first and most important step in improving your self-esteem is to actively move to accomplish and realize things you don't like about yourself that can be changed and to just as forcefully make yourself quit worrying about those things that cannot be changed. You will feel better about yourself for actually doing something positive to upgrade your self-image and also for exercising the strength of character to forget about things over which you have no control.

Who Do You Think You Are?

It may sound deceptively simple and pat but it can and does work wonders. When the widowed Kaye took her first step toward doing something for herself instead of waiting for someone else or something else to make things better, it ignited a sequence of other positive steps which restored her happiness and self-esteem. It opens the door to admit, possibly for the first time in years, the small but cumulatively essential self-affirmations needed to rebuild your pride and self-respect.

Positive Steps

1. *Get healthy.* To feel good about yourself, you first have to feel good physically. It is a scientific fact that the mind can affect health. Research in the field of stress has demonstrated that the opposite is also true: feeling better physically can affect the mind, and thus your self-esteem.

It certainly helps physical self-esteem to be fit and trim, but it is not just a matter of appearance. It is rather a total sense of health and well-being that is needed.

"If you are sick, tired, unattractive, whose fault is it?" challenges 73-year-old California fitness Guru Jack LaLanne. "There is only one person that accounts for you, and that's you.

"Habits, habits, habits. That's what it's all about," he said in a recent interview. He recommends walking in combination with other exercises but insists that the key is getting off the couch and sticking with a nutritious diet.

"You'd be surprised what can happen in just 30 days if you just do something about it."

2. *Be self-affirming.* Instead of focusing constantly on your shortcomings and failings, think about all your strong points and accomplishments.

Misers count and recount their money. Investors add up their net worth almost daily. You should do the same with yourself. Are you good with people? Do you have a sharp memory? Are you patient and effective at work or in crises? These are pluses and I'll bet you have a bundle of them if you stop and think about it. What about all the things you can do? Make a list and don't leave anything off of it. Everything, big and little, is an asset—from being a good cook to sailing a boat; from being good with your hands to being a whiz at bridge.

3. *Be self-congratulatory.* Nothing bolsters us quite so much as a pat on the back from others. "Great job!" "How did you manage that?" "Only you could have pulled that off."

The trouble is that it can be a long time between such much-deserved compliments. Sometimes other people simply take the good job you have done for granted; sometimes there is nobody around to appreciate your achievement—and it is often quite an achievement simply to get through the day's routine.

Who Do You Think You Are?

There is no reason not to give yourself a word of praise, to stop and say to yourself, "Not bad, not bad at all." Too few of us take time to congratulate ourselves on our patience, endurance, special efforts, and skills. Start handing out your own bouquets and blue ribbons to a self that deserves them. And, while you cannot give yourself a raise, you can provide a bonus now and then. Give yourself a special dinner or buy something frivolous that you've been wanting.

Let's hear it for you—from you!

4. *Get involved: be a volunteer.* An effective antidote for low self-esteem is the pride one can take in serving the needs of others as a volunteer. An additional bonus is the comradeship provided by fellow workers and the appreciation of the individuals you help. In their eyes you are definitely somebody special. And you are.

According to a *New York Times* article, "As some 89 million Americans have already discovered and researchers have documented, volunteering can enhance self-esteem, foster a sense of accomplishment and competence and act as an antidote to stress and depressions. In fact, some studies have shown that people who volunteer their services tend to be healthier and happier and live longer than those who do not volunteer."

5. *Specialize in something.* Make yourself good, really good, at some one thing. It really does not matter what it is so long as it interests, challenges and in-

volves you. Become an expert bird watcher, a gourmet cook, an authority on local history, a ham radio operator, a skilled wood-worker, a seamstress or weaver, a maven on the Middle East. The point is to be better at what you are into than anybody else you know, not in a spirit of competition or to be able to brag, but simply for the intense self-satisfaction that being really good at something brings.

Of course, it won't hurt your sense of self-esteem if you can quietly display your expertise for others from time to time.

6. *Be your own judge.* Appoint yourself Chief Justice of your own life. No matter what the evidence others—or circumstances—may bring against your self-esteem, realize that no one can condemn or demean you but yourself. Judges very rarely are put on trial and they always have the power to say, "Case dismissed."

Don't Be Afraid to Seek Counseling

This book, and others that are listed in the section on "Helpful Reading" which follows, will prove, I hope, beneficial to those who want to understand both the ways in which the self-esteem we should all feel for ourselves can be destroyed and rebuilt. But there are cases where esteem has been driven so low by destructive conditions that professional counselling by a psychologist or psychiatrist is definitely required.

Who Do You Think You Are?

Do not be ashamed or frightened to seek such professional help. Be assured that you are not the only one who suffers. Clinics and professionals do not establish themselves simply in the hope that you might some day turn to them. They are there because so many people need them and turn to them. It is foolish to continue in pain when help like this is as close as the yellow pages in your phone book.

Conclusion

The quest for self-understanding as a key to human happiness and fulfillment is not new. Over the gates to the Delphic Oracle in ancient Greece were carved the words:

Know Thyself

The aim of this book is to put you back in touch with the unique being and personality that is your real self—not a self-image that has been imposed by others. Because, as the title suggests, who you think you are makes all the difference in life. Once you fully understand and accept your real self, this phrase should be carved in stone over the gateway to your mind:

Accept Thyself

And that means without reservations, because as we have seen, you cannot be, and should not wish to be, anyone other than yourself.

And finally engrave the words:

Esteem Thyself

While it is true, as actor Rod Steiger says that "the most important thing is to be *whatever* you are without

Joel Wells

shame,'' it is just as important to be *everything* you can be with pride in who you are, because of who you are.

It is not a question of whether you can be somebody. You are somebody.

Some Helpful Reading

The Ann Landers Encyclopedia—A to Z
see "Self-Esteem," pp. 952-954
Doubleday

How to Raise Your Self-Esteem
Honoring the Self
The Psychology of Self-Esteem
all by Nathaniel Brandon, Ph.D.
Bantam Books

Codependent No More:
How to Stop Controlling Others and Start Caring
for Yourself
by Melody Beattie
Harper/Hazeldon

"I ain't much, baby—but I'm all I've got."
by Jess Lair, Ph.D.
Fawcett Crest

Celebrate Your Self:
Enhancing Your Own Self-Esteem
by Dorothy Corkville Briggs
Doubleday

Joel Wells

Compassion and Self-Hate:
An Alternative to Despair
by Theodore Isaac Rubin, M.D.
Collier Macmillan

Feeling Good: The New Mood Therapy
by David M. Burns, M.D.
Signet/New American Library

Identity, Youth and Crisis
by Erik H. Erickson
W.W. Norton

Between Parent and Child
by H. Ginott
Macmillan

Coping in the 80s:
Eliminating Needless Stress and Guilt
by Joel Wells
Thomas More Press

Woman's Workshop is a quarterly newsletter which its publishers say "is designed to speak to three groups of women: full-time mothers who have never had a career; sequencers, who have given up careers to rear children but plan to return to work; and women who consider motherhood a full-time career but need to work part-time for financial reasons. We want to focus

Who Do You Think You Are?

on women as people rather than as mothers.'' The newsletter is $16 per year. Subscriptions: P.O. Box 843, Coronado, CA 92118

Your Aging Parents
by John Deedy
Thomas More Press